BRANSON
COOKIN' COUNTRY

BRANSON
COOKIN' COUNTRY

FEATURING

RESTAURANTS
AND RECIPES
FROM AMERICA'S
COUNTRY MUSIC
CAPITAL

SUSAN ST. MARIE-MARTIN

TWO LANE PRESS, INC.

ISBN 1-878686-13-5

Printed in the United States of America

Text and cover design: Calvert Guthrie
Editor: Jane Doyle Guthrie
Food consultant: Judith Fertig

10 9 8 7 6 5 4 3 2 1   93 94 95 96 97

Two Lane Press, Inc.
4245 Walnut Street
Kansas City, MO 64111
(816) 531-3119

To my children, Sabrina and Ryan,
the two greatest blessings God has given me.
And to "Trickie"; you are, and I love you for it.

CONTENTS

ACKNOWLEDGMENTS

When choosing the restaurants for this book, I relied heavily on suggestions and recommendations. I would like to thank the countless number of strangers who allowed me to accost them with such questions as, "Did you enjoy your meal?" "Was the service good?" "Would you eat here again?" Many bushels of gratitude go to each individual I wrote about here, for both taking time out of a busy tourist season to talk with me and sharing their highly guarded and treasured recipes.

I would like to specifically thank the following people: Peter Herschend, Executive Vice Chairman of Silver Dollar City, Inc., and Roger Walters, Director of Corporate Planning for Silver Dollar City, who moved mountains and enabled us to move to Branson; Mike and Colleen Zirbel, who opened many doors for me in Branson; David Baker at Banta Foods, for letting me pick his brain; Betty Beasley, for sharing her wonderful memories of the cast of the "Beverly Hillbillies"; and Margaret Frimml, who purchased the first copy of this cookbook, sight unseen.

Last, I would like to thank my husband Jim, the walking calculator, for not complaining when I woke him at 2 A.M. asking for help in converting measurements. Also for feeding the children vegetables instead of hot dogs while I wrote.

To these people and many more . . . thank you and may God bless you.

Branson Cookin' Country offers you more than a fine variety of recipes. The restaurants featured are an eclectic blend of fine cuisine and the "mom and pop" diners that so typify the diversification of Ozark mountain country.

Susan has captured the very essence of this in her book. Each recipe, restaurant, and person she has included is as varied as the music to be found here.

Peter F. Herschend
Vice Chairman
Silver Dollar City, Inc.

There is something magical about the Branson area that even as a writer I find difficult to describe. The Ozark Mountains, as old as they are, overflow with life. There is music in the air that isn't an echo from the many theaters along Highway 76. There is a special glow in the sky that isn't a reflection from the lights that illuminate Branson's famous strip at night. There is a peacefulness here despite the seemingly endless line of traffic congesting the streets of the town now billed the "Country Music Capital of the Universe." However, the theaters, the strip, and, yes, even the traffic are all a part of the magic that makes this area so exquisitely wonderful.

The population of Branson hovers a little over 3,700. Yet in any given week between the months of April and December, the number of visitors explodes this tiny dot on the map. People from across the U.S., indeed from around the world, come to see the small and the great, the famous and the not so famous, who are making their mark in our small town.

The marquees above the theaters read like a celebrity "Who's Who." The Grand Palace, Branson's largest theater, which can hold the entire population of Branson and then some, hosts a myriad of top entertainers like John Denver, Anne Murray, Reba McIntire, and Ronnie Milsap, as well as featuring the multitalented Glen Campbell as a regular host. Country legends like Ray Stevens, Mel Tillis, Roy Clark, Mickey Gilley, Jim Stafford, Moe Bandy, Buck Trent, and Box Car Willie perform nightly in their own theaters. Other renowned country celebrities perform as regular guests at others. Andy Williams, Shoji Tabuchi, the Osmond Brothers, Tony Orlando, and Wayne Newton have each opened a theater and enhanced Branson with their own unique sounds. Of course no list would be complete without noting the exceptional talents of the groups that started it all, such as the Baldknobbers, the Presleys, and the Foggy River Boys. These entertainers and others perform for literally millions of visitors annually.

Besides the theaters, there are world class attractions that entice visitors to the area. Silver Dollar City, undoubtedly one of the most beautiful and friendly theme parks in America, attracts close to 2 million visitors a year. The park hosts a huge and beautifully displayed annual craft fair in the fall. From the middle of November through December, the Old Time Country Christmas celebration illuminates the park in a dazzling display of lights as the entire area celebrates Ozark Mountain Christmas.

Shepherd of the Hills, long known for its outdoor drama based on the novel by Harold Bell Wright, evokes the serene beauty and tranquility that early settlers found as their covered wagons topped the first breathtaking Ozark peak and they surveyed the rich green valleys below. Visitors today can recapture that awesome vista from high atop Inspiration Tower.

Ride the Ducks, a land/water ride, offers visitors a spectacular tour that includes a "duck's-eye view" of magnificent Table Rock Lake. The Lake Queen cruises our other beautiful lake, Taneycomo, with music and dining accompaniments. Numerous other attractions include Waltzing Waters, Stone Hill Winery, Mutton Hollow, Talking Rock Caverns, and the ever-popular helicopter rides.

As for shopping, Branson is unsurpassed in quaint and unique shops, most featuring the talents of local artisans. If you're a serious bargain hunter, the Factory Merchants Mall is a trip to heaven.

But the main ingredient shaping Branson into the present phenomenon rests with the inhabitants themselves. The sincerity in the people of this community is apparent everywhere. When they say "Glad to meet you," they mean it. They look you in the eye when they talk and have a ready and easy smile for strangers on the street. They maintain the stubborn determination that Missourians have long been known for and a predisposition for honesty, integrity, and ingenuity.

Although intended first and foremost as a cookbook, this volume offers an eclectic assortment of recipes, restaurants, and stories about the uncanny individuals that operate them. Many are Ozark natives carrying on a proud family tradition, some arrived from other parts of Missouri to forge new enterprises along Highway 76, but most are newcomers, bent on maintaining our proud Missouri tradition. A few even came here to retire and instead found themselves embarking on new careers! Of course, there are the entrepreneurs who came seeking fame and fortune, but unlike explorers of old, they've reinvested their wealth in the community from which it came.

The recipes collected here present a melodic blend of appetizers, entrees, and delicious desserts. One was written on a bit of paper and hand-carried to America centuries ago. Another has been a family tradition for three generations. One is even the result of a mistake made while talking on the phone.

The restaurants range from elegant fine-dining establishments to a one-stool ice cream parlor/bookstore, but all typify the Branson area. Although many specialize in Ozark-style country cooking, others feature unpronounceable menu items with an unforgettable taste. Some prepare delicious steaks while others whip together superb sandwiches. A portion pride themselves on having the best buffet in town, while others stress the fact that they offer no buffet at all. Though some have been an integral part of Branson for many years, those in operation only a short time are nonetheless important to sampling the area "cuisine."

Because Branson is primarily a resort area, much of the attraction is the constant state of change; people and places come and go as do the seasons. If, at some point, you choose to dine at one of the restaurants featured here and find that it has changed management or even closed its doors, the recipe still remains tried and true and perhaps one day will become part of your family's history.

RESTAURANTS & RECIPES

Note: The last line in the restaurant information that appears at the bottom of each recipe contains the following "shorthand": $ (under $10); $$ ($10 to $20); $$$ ($20 and up); □ (credit cards accepted); no □ (credit cards not accepted); C (casual); D (dressy). The final element in this coding system, a number in parentheses, refers to the restaurant location, which is keyed to the map at the back of this book.

Entering Ahoys transports the visitor back in time to an 1800s New England lighthouse. Oars, ropes, and other rigging, remnants of an old fishing boat, hang on the walls. The floors creak when you walk and, if you use your imagination, you can almost hear the sound of the waves crashing against the shore. Set off in an alcove is a life-size painting of a weathered old seafarer who seems to follow you with his eyes.

The nautically themed Ahoys is a family restaurant specializing in (what else?) seafood. It's one of the few places in the area where you can get boiled crawfish, a dozen of the little critters per order, served with a zesty cocktail sauce. The specialty of the house is frog legs, deep fried and delicious and available as an appetizer or entree. The menu also features grilled fish and jumbo shrimp flown in daily from the Gulf. The children's menu includes all-time favorites like hamburgers, hot dogs, chicken nuggets, plus the ever-popular grilled cheese sandwich.

Ahoys' lounge offers many exotic drinks to complement the seafood selections. After just one of the original concoctions called "Jamaica Me Crazy," you feel like you could fly to the island under your own power.

Built in 1982, the restaurant originally was called "The Fishin' Shack." A meat smoker used to sit where the fireplace now stands. While the smell was delicious, the smoke pouring forth was not conducive to enjoyable dining. When Jim Christenson acquired the property several years ago, he promptly replaced the smoker with a fireplace and changed the restaurant's name. He also added an outdoor dining patio overlooking Table Rock Lake.

Ahoys is a popular gathering place for Kimberling City locals as well as a favorite spot to celebrate birthdays, anniversaries, and other special occasions. One of the niceties offered the honored guest is a personalized menu cover commemorating the event.

Another reason for this restaurant's popularity is that it is one of the handful of dining establishments on Table Rock Lake that diners can reach by means other than their cars. A customer docking facility, located about a hundred yards from the front door, has been provided for boaters' convenience.

Whether you arrive by land or by lake, dine inside or out, you'll always be assured of good food, good service, and a good time at Ahoys.

Crab Salad Ahoy

8 ounces imitation crabmeat
1/2 cup mayonnaise
1/4 cup sour cream
1/4 cup sliced green onions
1/4 cup chopped celery
1 hard-boiled egg, chopped
1/2 tablespoon lemon juice
2 teaspoons dill weed
1/2 teaspoon pepper

Thoroughly combine all ingredients and serve chilled. (*Note:* Make a day ahead to allow flavors to combine.)

Serves 8–10

AHOYS
Kimberling Inn Resort and Conference Center
Highway 13, Kimberling City Shopping Center
Kimberling City, MO 65686
(417) 739-4311
$–$$; □; C; (10)

On a high hill overlooking a lush valley below stands one of Branson's foremost attractions, The Shepherd of the Hills. There are no wild rides here except when one of the horses kicks up a ruckus. In the setting of a peaceful 1800s village stands a white clapboard church, a working mill, and quaint shops in which to browse. The 230-foot Inspiration Tower, a Branson landmark, offers a view that, on a clear day, extends up to 90 miles in all directions.

Harold Bell Wright published his *Shepherd of the Hills* in 1907. Soon visitors started pouring in to acquaint themselves with the amazing people and tranquil area about which this gentle man had written. One of the people characterized in the novel was a woman everyone called Aunt Mollie. A kind-hearted soul, she was the epitome of an Ozark-country woman; unperturbable in the face of danger and amiable to all. One would often find Aunt Mollie working in her kitchen, preparing a country feast for neighbors and friends. Thus it was appropriate to name the restaurant located on the Shepherd of the Hills property "Aunt Mollie's Cupboard."

Aunt Mollie would heartily approve of the establishment's design. Homey early-American booths and tables and chairs sit comfortably on a hardwood floor. Chintz curtains flutter in a spring breeze offering an overall feeling of friendliness. The restaurant's namesake also would approve of the buffet (there is no menu service), where folks can eat as much as they want in a leisurely manner.

Being a fine cook herself, Aunt Mollie would delight in the lavish spread. The regular variety of delicious entrees often includes a scrumptious beef stroganoff simmering in a thick brown gravy and a delectable mushroom chicken, as much of a treat as the fried catfish, coated in a secret combination of spices. Basic salad choices such as potato, coleslaw, and a creamy macaroni are designed to appease every taste. Desserts, all baked fresh in the kitchen, include a flaky peach or blackberry cobbler, a moist carrot cake, and a plump apple or pumpkin pie.

The Shepherd of the Hills is a family operation, and from the moment you walk on the property, you're treated like a visiting relation. Owners Gary and Pat Snadon have incorporated the vast talents of their two daughters, Sharena and Shawna, into the everyday running of the park. Even son-in-law Doug has been tapped as Assistant General Manager.

Gary purchased the property in 1986, when the only incentive to visit was the famous "Shepherd of the Hills" outdoor drama established in 1956. It was his desire to offer visitors a taste of what first drew attention to the area, so he created an attraction that would allow them to literally step back in time.

The Shepherd of the Hills offers a truly delightful way to spend a day. And if you see a tiny woman, hair pulled back in a bun and serene face covered with an easy smile, it's probably Aunt Mollie just making sure that you're having a good time.

Shepherd's Pie

2-1/2 cups plus 1/3 cup Bisquick
2/3 cup milk
2-1/2 pounds ground beef
1/8 cup diced yellow onion
6 tablespoons Worcestershire
   sauce
3/4 cup tomato sauce
Salt and pepper to taste
2 eggs
3-3/4 cups shredded cheddar
   cheese

Pour 2-1/2 cups Bisquick into a large bowl and slowly add milk. Mix to a soft dough. Transfer dough to a lightly floured work surface and gently roll into a ball. Knead dough 5 or 6 times. Roll out dough about 2 inches wider than a 1-1/2-quart casserole dish. Arrange dough in dish, using a fork to edge crust.

Preheat oven to 350 degrees. Brown ground beef in a large skillet. Drain off fat and add onions to skillet. Cook over medium heat until onions are tender. Stir in 1/3 cup Bisquick, Worcestershire sauce, tomato sauce, salt, and pepper. Continue stirring for about 1 minute, then spoon into prepared pie crust.

Break eggs into a mixing bowl and beat with a wire whisk. Add cheddar cheese and mix thoroughly. Pour over meat mixture in crust. Cover pie loosely with foil to prevent excessive browning. Bake on middle rack in oven for 25 minutes. Remove foil and bake for another 5 minutes.

Serves 4–6

AUNT MOLLIE'S CUPBOARD
West Highway 76
HCR 1, Box 770
Branson, MO 65616
(417) 334-4191
$; □; C; (3)

B & G BOOKS & MORE

This little establishment, located at East Highway 160 and Kissee Mills Junction, is well worth the effort required to find it. It is run by three of the finest, down home people you would ever want to meet.

When the visitor walks in, Barbara Amos, her daughter Diane, and a gathering of the locals will probably be sitting around the single kitchen table discussing politics or Barbara's favorite subject, cooking. Barbara's husband Glen will intersperse the conversation with his wry sense of humor and meander out the door. His pearls of wisdom are well worth remembering and taking for your own.

As the name implies, this is a bookstore with over 7,000 well-read volumes from which to choose, all categorized and stowed in their proper places on the shelves. It's also an ice cream shop, specializing in the most delectable sodas ever sipped through a straw. This somewhat strange combination came about through Barbara's love of books and a dream of serving up quality ice cream parlor delicacies.

"I don't skimp on syrup or flavoring," says Barbara. "I use the best ice cream available and each soda is topped with whipping cream, sprinkles, and a cherry! Never once have I had anyone ask for more chocolate."

The Amos family first visited the area in 1956 while on vacation. "We'd stay at the White Swan Motel for $4.00 a night," recalls Glen. "If we stayed over and they didn't have to change the sheets, they'd only charge us $2.00 for the second night."

Barbara and Glen moved to Forsyth in 1986. Already having established a reputation in the area as a superb baker, requests for her pies, cakes, cinnamon rolls, and fresh bread brought Barbara almost more business than she could handle. Meanwhile, her book collection had grown to a staggering 7,209. As she recalls, "Glen said, 'Honey, we've got to do something with these things,' so he built me this building and I put my books in here and opened up my ice cream place."

Barbara's baked goods are not displayed bakery style; each one is created from scratch upon request. "If someone wants a pie, a cake, or loaf of bread, all they have to do is call me. I get calls from ladies every day asking me to bake something for them," Barbara says. "Sometimes with no more than two hours' notice. I just run everyone out of my kitchen and whip up something special for them."

One of her specialties is a black oil cake made with heavenly fudge icing and marshmallow topping. Another, which she calls Barbara's Mistake, is a coffee cake chock full of juicy, ripe peaches or cherries.

B & G Books & More is indeed more, a whole lot more. You can spend hours browsing through thousands of volumes, catch up on the latest gossip over an ice cream soda, or just sit and enjoy the company.

Dixie Pie

3 eggs
1 cup light corn syrup
1 cup sugar
3 tablespoons melted butter
3 tablespoons flour
1/2 teaspoon salt
1-1/2 cups chopped English
    walnuts
1/2 cup chocolate chips

Preheat oven to 450 degrees. Beat eggs thoroughly. Add corn syrup, sugar, butter, flour, and salt, and mix well. Stir in walnuts and chocolate chips and mix well. Pour mixture into an uncooked **No-Fail Pie Crust**. Place on center rack and bake for 15 minutes. Reduce heat to 350 degrees and bake for about 25 minutes more, until done.

Serves 6–8

No-Fail Pie Crust

1/2 cup vegetable oil
5 tablespoons ice water
2 cups sifted flour
1/2 teaspoon salt

(Note: Measurements *must* be exact.) Whisk together oil and ice water. Add flour and salt and knead mixture thoroughly. Moisten work surface and cover with waxed paper. Transfer dough to waxed paper and cover with another sheet of waxed paper. Roll dough out to approximately 10 inches in diameter. Remove top sheet of paper and place pie pan face down on dough. Flip pan and dough over using bottom sheet of waxed paper. Remove paper, then trim and pinch crust around edges. (Note: If recipe calls for a cooked crust, preheat oven to 350 degrees. Prick bottom of crust with a fork 4 or 5 times. Place on center rack in oven and bake for 15 minutes or until brown.)

Makes 1 (9-inch) pie crust

B & G BOOKS & MORE
Corner of East Highway 160 and Kissee Mills Junction
HCR 3, Box 48
Forsyth, MO 65653
(417) 546-6901
$; no □; C; (12)

BIG JIM'S STEAK HOUSE

Judging from outside appearances, this restaurant might remind you of a saloon found in Dodge City, when outlaws were tough and Marshal Dillon was the law. You might even hesitate for a moment about going in on the chance that Black Bart might be inside, drinking beer and in one of his mean moods. However, once inside you'll discover that taking this step into the past became one of the best decisions you've ever made.

You'll find families seated at red-and-white-checked tables and fresh-faced teens sharing a cozy canopied booth. A voice from the kitchen may yell, "Just sit anywhere you want, hon," so choose one of the comfy booths. No sooner are you seated than a waitress brings you a basket of freshly popped popcorn and a typed menu in a plastic sleeve.

Big Jim's is a no-frills restaurant, but you'll find the food and service some of the best anywhere. The steaks, prepared with Big Jim's own secret sauce, and the walleye, breaded with Jim's own coating recipe, are out of this world. As a matter of fact, each portion of the meal, from the homemade ranch dressing (yummm!) to the side dish of fried potatoes and onions, is delicious.

Chicago transplant "Big Jim" Spizewski had always been interested in cooking but got his first real break while working as a bartender for a kosher catering company. "I wasn't much of a bartender," says Jim, "but I sure knew my way around a kitchen. Before long, this Pole had become a kosher chef."

Soon after leaving the catering company, Jim packed up his family and moved to Stone Ridge, Missouri. He bought the Ozark Mountain Pub, which at the time had a "rough" reputation, and changed the name, hoping to attract a family-oriented clientele. He replaced the pool table by the front door with dining tables and evicted the rowdies. Jim "decorated" the place himself with his own mounted fish and a huge collection of painted saw blades. ("I've even done some remodeling," he grins. "I painted the floors.")

Specialties of the house include steaks, "good and tender" (try the hefty 20-ounce T-bone, cooked any way you like it); breaded walleye and catfish; homemade pizzas piled high with three varieties of cheese; and fried chicken gizzards. Every Friday and Saturday night a live rockabilly band entertains while Big Jim prepares meals in his five-foot by three-foot kitchen. ("How much room do you need to cook a steak?" he asks.)

Big Jim's Steak House is located on Highway 13 in Stone Ridge about 30 minutes from downtown Branson, and it's well worth the drive.

Big Jim's Wash and Coating Mix

1 egg
4 cups milk
4 tablespoons lemon juice
3 tablespoons Tabasco sauce
4 cups flour
1 cup bread crumbs
1 cup cornmeal
3 tablespoons pepper
3 tablespoons seasoned salt
3 tablespoons garlic powder
2 tablespoons oregano
2 tablespoons celery salt

In a large bowl, combine egg, milk, lemon juice, and Tabasco. Set aside. In second bowl combine flour, bread crumbs, cornmeal, pepper, seasoned salt, garlic, oregano, and celery salt. Dip meat in liquid wash, then dredge in dry mix, making sure piece is covered. Lay on waxed paper and freeze for 60 to 90 minutes. (This will help the coating stay on while cooking.)

Deep-fry meat in oil at 375 degrees until golden brown. (Note: Excellent for fish, poultry, or pork. Coating mix will keep in freezer for up to 30 days.)

Makes enough to coat 15 to 20 pieces of meat

BIG JIM'S STEAK HOUSE
Highway 13 North
Stone Ridge, MO 65737
(417) 739-2125
$-$$; no □; C; (9)

BOB EVANS GENERAL STORE

The name "Bob Evans" has been synonymous with sausage ever since he opened his first restaurant in Gallipolis, Ohio, in 1946. Today Bob Evans Farms, Inc. operates nearly 270 family restaurants in a six-state area. In the spring of 1991, Bob Evans General Store opened its doors in Branson near the intersection of Highways 65 and 76 west. The proprietors have enjoyed a tremendous success, thanks in part to the delicious home-cooked food and the family-budget prices.

Everyone knows that Bob Evans serves up a walloping-good breakfast, and with over twenty items to choose from, you're sure to find something to tempt your taste buds. The Country Skillet Breakfast is a tasty combination of eggs, sliced potatoes, and sausage, topped with gravy and shredded cheese. The accompanying baked apples and biscuits round out this hearty selection. The Sausage Hash Casserole is a savory combination of green and red peppers, potatoes, and sausage, smothered in a special sauce and capped off with a zesty American cheese.

If you spent breakfast browsing through the general store, pop in for lunch and try one of the delicious homemade sandwiches or salads. If you did skip breakfast and want something more substantial, there are five "Early American" meals to choose from, such as the perpetually popular fried chicken and a scrumptious chicken potpie. Pinto beans are a traditional favorite, and Bob's are among the very best. Served with all-you-can-eat, light and fluffy corn muffins, it's hard to say no even when they bring around the third basketful.

The restaurant staff is friendly and accommodating and the person who keeps them on their toes is general manager Doug Kissenger. A transplant from Green Bay, Wisconsin (he'll be happy to spend hours discussing the Packers with you), he came to work for Bob Evans in 1989 and hasn't regretted a day.

"The Branson store is the third new restaurant that I've opened for the company," says Doug. "They've given me the opportunity to work in different parts of the country, but of all the places I've been, I like Branson the best. I just hope they let me stay here for a while."

When you visit Bob Evans General Store, you'll want to stay for a while, too. And as Bob Evans himself has often been quoted as saying, "You're always welcomed, so come often and stay as long as you can."

Bob Evans General Store Meatloaf

1-1/3 pounds ground beef
1-1/3 pounds sausage
2 tablespoons vegetable oil
1/2 cup diced onions
1/2 cup diced celery
2 eggs
1/3 cup ketchup
1/3 cup picante sauce
1/8 teaspoon garlic powder
3/4 cup dried bread crumbs

Preheat oven to 350 degrees. Sauté onions and celery in oil until tender, the remove from pan and rinse with water. Drain well and set aside.

Beat eggs rapidly for 30 seconds. Add ketchup, picante sauce, and garlic powder. Mix rapidly for 30 seconds, scrape bowl, and blend for another 30 seconds. Add onions, celery, ground beef, and sausage to mixture. Blend slowly for 1 minute. Scrape bowl and add bread crumbs. Mix for 1 minute.

Press meat firmly and evenly into a medium loaf pan. Round all edges so excess fat can drain off top of loaf while baking. Cover with foil and bake for approximately 75 minutes. Remove from pan immediately and cut into 3/4-inch slices.

Serves 8

BOB EVANS GENERAL STORE
801 West Main Street
Branson, MO 65616
(417) 336-2023
$; □; C; (2)

BRANSON CAFE

In the early 1900s, Branson was a quiet little community with a few shops, a busy boarding house, and the Branson Cafe, where everyone gathered to catch up on the latest happenings. In 1912, while the men were off at a hanging in Stone County, a fire devastated the entire town. When the smoke had cleared and the tears had dried, the undaunted people of Branson rebuilt it from the ground up! Some of the shopkeepers moved on, but the cafe soon reopened for business, hosting notables like Rose O'Neill, Harold Bell Wright of *Shepherd of the Hills* fame, and world-renowned artist Thomas Hart Benton.

Today, Branson is still a quiet community despite the millions of visitors that enter its city limits each year. Numerous new and trendy restaurants have been opened to accommodate the influx, but the ever-popular Branson Cafe has remained much the same as it was in 1912, including the good old-fashioned, home-style cooking. Everything is made from scratch in the small kitchen. The chicken-fried steak and pork tenderloin are battered in a delicious coating, with meat so tender you can cut it with your fork.

The cafe's hamburgers undoubtedly are among the best in the area. Made of ground beef delivered fresh daily, they are thick and juicy and served on toasted buns. The specialty here is the deep-fried chicken, and the cafe boasts, "If the Colonel had our recipe, he would be a general now." The breakfast menu offers something for every appetite, including light and fluffy pecan pancakes and homemade biscuits smothered in a thick ham gravy.

Owner Ken Roten's family moved to Branson in 1959 from Freistatt, Missouri, while his wife Joan (pronounced "JoAnne") is a fifth-generation native. "We're still newcomers compared to her family," jokes Ken.

Both Ken and Joan come from families of great cooks. When they bought the cafe in 1985, they turned it into a family affair. Ken's father George, a baker of considerable repute, comes in early every morning to begin making the wonderful assortment of pies, cobblers, biscuits, and hot rolls served in the restaurant. His mother, Betty, works part time as the cashier and handles the catering along with Joan's mother and father. During the summer, their two children can be found busing tables and carrying on a delightful repartee with the customers.

Ken credits his employees for most of his success. But whether it's the employees themselves or the delicious home-cooking they serve, eating at the Branson Cafe will make any trip to the area memorable.

Easy Hot Yeast Rolls

2 cups milk
1/2 cup yeast
8 cups flour
1/3 cup sugar
1/2 teaspoon salt
1/3 cup shortening
4 eggs
Melted butter

Warm milk slightly. Add yeast to milk and set aside.

In a large bowl, combine flour, sugar, salt, shortening, and eggs. Mix well, add milk, and knead mixture into dough. Pinch off a piece of dough about half the size of an egg. Roll it into a ball and place it into a lightly oiled, square cake pan. Repeat process until pan has been filled. (Balls should be close together but not touching.) Fill second oiled cake pan with remaining dough, rolled according to directions.

Cover cake pan with a dish towel and place on top of oven while preheating to 350 degrees. Let rolls rise until they reach the top of the pan. Remove towel and place pan on the middle rack of the oven. Bake for 15 minutes or until golden brown. Remove from oven and brush tops with melted butter or margarine.

Serves 8–12

BRANSON CAFE
120 West Main Street
Branson, MO 65616
(417) 334-3021
$; □; C; (1)

THE BRASS RAIL

The Brass Rail Restaurant has become one of the favorite after-work gathering places in the Branson area. Located on West Highway 76 half a mile west of Silver Dollar City in the Best Western Mountain Oak Lodge, it's a convenient stop off for commuters living in the satellite communities. In addition to a well-stocked lounge, this congenial spot offers a delicious yet inexpensive buffet.

The dinner buffet features three varied but always delicious entree selections. The beef brisket, bathed in a thick rich barbecue sauce, always wins the people's choice award. However, when the charbroiled pork chops appear, seldom do any remain at the end of the evening. There is always a big kettle of soup, and a salad bar resplendent with fresh vegetables. Each morning a breakfast buffet entices diners with hot, homemade biscuits, patty or link sausages, bacon, ham, and fluffy scrambled eggs.

The menu offers a wide selection of entrees and sandwiches, including a great Reuben that tastes like it came from a New York deli. The seafood platter presents a huge portion of shrimp, scallops, and fish, deep-fried to perfection.

Manager Elaine Cler prides herself on the efficiency of her restaurant staff. Over twenty-three years of experience in the restaurant business have taught her a lot. "I've done everything from busing tables to line cooking," says Elaine. "Over the years one tried-and-true lesson that I have learned is that no matter how good the food is, if the service is bad or the waitresses are indifferent, people won't return." Every one of her hand-picked waitresses is friendly and chatty, and by the end of the meal you feel more like a visiting relative than a tourist.

There are other reasons to visit The Brass Rail besides the price, convenience, and hospitality. Within this bright, cheery restaurant, huge picture windows frame a splendid view of beautiful Ozark woods. Parties of six can request "The Pink Room," where, seated around an old oak table complemented by a matching sideboard, you feel like you're dining in your own home.

The Brass Rail hosts numerous tour groups and parties. Elaine's most requested menu is a beautiful almond-crusted chicken, succulent beef tenderloin with mushroom sauce, twice-baked potatoes covered in cheese, and black cherry crêpes.

If you're looking for a good, reasonably priced, and exceptionally friendly place to eat, try The Brass Rail. After paying the check, you'll still have money to spend in the lobby gift shop.

Elaine's Almond-Crusted Chicken

6 boneless, skinless chicken breast halves
2 eggs
1/2 cup milk
1 cup flour
2 cups crushed almonds
1/4 cup vegetable oil

Pound chicken breasts out flat. Thoroughly mix egg and milk together. Dredge chicken in flour, then dip in egg and milk mixture. Next firmly press both sides in crushed almonds. Place chicken in skillet with heated oil and fry both sides over medium heat until done (about 20 minutes). Pour *Amaretto Cream Sauce* over chicken prior to serving.

Serves 6–8

Amaretto Cream Sauce

1 quart whipping cream
1/3 cup Amaretto

Mix whipping cream and Amaretto in a saucepan. Bring mixture to a boil, stirring constantly, and cook until it turns thick and becomes a caramel color. Keep warm until ready to serve.

Makes about 4 cups

THE BRASS RAIL
West Highway 76
Branson, MO 65616
(417) 338-2141
$–$$; □; C; (7)

BRIER PATCH VILLAGE

Highway 13 is a picturesque two lane road composed of innumerable "S" curves. Snugly nestled in one of those curves in Stone Ridge is Brier Patch Village. The building looks like a Victorian manor complete with a gabled roof and lace curtains at the bay windows. Inside, the mixed scents of potpourri and freshly baked pastries recall memories of your grandmother's house. Homemade pies, cakes, cinnamon rolls, and cookies can be purchased in the bakery and offer an overwhelming temptation to sample every one.

The person responsible for most of this delicious pastry assortment is head baker Martha Benedict, who learned the art of baking sitting on a stool at her mother's elbow. Most of her recipes, such as her sticky buns, came to America with the first Mennonites in the early 1700s and have been passed down to her through generations.

The restaurant is bright, cheery, and homey, with ceiling fans circulating the fresh-baked smell. Brier Patch Village offers breakfast, lunch, and dinner, and each meal is a delight. Menu items run the gamut, from homemade Belgian waffles smothered in strawberries at breakfast to rolled fillet of sole stuffed with broccoli at dinner. The luncheon menu features daily specials such as chicken-fried steak covered with the best white gravy you've ever eaten. One of the favorite specials is a huge tomato stuffed with tuna accompanied by a homemade apple muffin.

The owners of Brier Patch Village, Ruthie and Jack Karr, moved to Stone Ridge from California with dreams of opening an upscale restaurant and bed and breakfast. They've succeeded at both.

The Victorian theme of the dining room, bakery, and gift shop carries into the second-floor guest rooms. Every bedroom is decorated in bright flowered chintz and period furniture.

The pièce de résistance, however, is called the Pink Room, which in no way adequately describes its appeal. Puffs of lace and pink satin canopy the king-size bed. Steps covered in plush dusty rose carpet lead up to a hot-pink hot tub bubbling enticingly in the corner. The outside door leads to a porch from which you get a breathtaking view of Table Rock Lake in the valley below. It's a perfect hideaway for a first, second, or even third honeymoon.

Brier Patch Village offers a delightful spot to visit on a pretty afternoon or a cozy place to curl up for the night. Ruthie and Jack are the perfect hosts, but with all those homemade pastries, they don't guarantee that you won't go away a few pounds heavier.

Sticky Buns

1 cup scalded milk
1 cup warm water
2 packages dry yeast
7 cups flour
1/2 cup (1 stick) margarine
1/2 cup sugar
1 teaspoon salt
2 eggs

Mix ingredients together well and knead until smooth. Cover and let dough rise until doubled (about 1 hour).

Preheat oven to 350 degrees. Place dough on a floured surface and roll out to a rectangle about 1/2-inch thick. Spread with **Dough Coating**, roll up jelly-roll fashion, and cut into 1-inch slices. Put 1 tablespoon of **Goo** in the bottom of each cup of 3 greased muffin tins. Add optional pecan halves if desired. Place dough slices, cut-side down, on top of **Goo**. Bake for 25 minutes or until brown. (Note: For cinnamon rolls, place 1-inch slices, cut-side down, on greased cookie sheets. Bake for 25 minutes or until brown. While hot, top with glaze made of 2 cups powdered sugar and just enough water to allow the glaze to drizzle over tops of cinnamon rolls.)

Makes about 36 buns

Dough Coating

1/2 cup melted margarine
1-1/2 cups firmly packed brown sugar
2 tablespoons cinnamon

Combine margarine with sugar and cinnamon, then set aside until ready to use.

Goo

1 cup firmly packed brown sugar
1 cup dark corn syrup
1/2 cup (1 stick) margarine
1 small package pecan halves (optional)

Combine ingredients in a saucepan. Bring to a boil, then set aside until ready to use.

BRIER PATCH VILLAGE
Highway 13
Stone Ridge, MO 65737
(417) 739-4150
$–$$; □; C; (9)

17

BUCK TRENT BREAKFAST THEATER

A fellow entertainer once said, "Buck Trent is a show in himself, on or off the stage." Very true. Even if Buck were not a world-class banjo player, he could entertain anyone with just his delightful sense of humor. Two things make going to the Buck Trent Breakfast Theater so enjoyable: witnessing firsthand the personable charm and super talents of this fine musician, and savoring a delicious, old-fashioned, Ozark-style breakfast while doing so.

Guests dine in the cozy theater, where crisp blue-and-white checked tablecloths cover each table. The breakfast buffet, which opens promptly at 8:00 A.M., is nothing fancy, but very inviting. Displayed in a country-kitchen setting, the offerings include delicious spicy sausage, thick slices of ham, hot homemade biscuits, thick tasty sausage gravy, fluffy scrambled eggs, and crispy hashbrowns. A trio of fruits may include sweet ripe cantaloupe or fresh juicy pineapple. Beverage choices are freshly brewed hot coffee, fragrant hot tea, or rich hot chocolate, perfect to warm you up for a cold winter morning performance.

The theater, located in Tommy's restaurant, is off Highway 65. Although housed in a building considered tiny when compared to most of the other theaters in Branson, the size definitely lends to the hominess found inside. Nita Delworth, who assists Buck and his wife Jean in running the theater, is the picture of Ozark hospitality. When Nita says "Enjoy yourself," you know she means it.

Jean Trent, as down to earth and unpretentious as they come, is always on hand to add that extra-special welcome. Still starry-eyed over Buck even after years of marriage, it was she who devised the breakfast show after his triple-bypass heart surgery in June 1992.

After the breakfast dishes have been cleared and the audience has enjoyed the talents of singing sensation Cindi Barr and the adorable Moore Brothers, Buck Trent takes the spotlight. Twice named "Instrumentalist of the Year" by the prestigious Country Music Association and recipient of other similar accolades, Buck has come a long way from his beginnings in Spartanburg, South Carolina. When he got his first regular job as a musician on "The Cousin Wilbur and Blondie Show" in Asheville, he called his mother and told her, "Mama, I've made the big time." It paid $40.00 a week.

The breakfast and show at Buck Trent's Breakfast Theater is one of the most enjoyable in Branson. Buck enjoys it so much himself that he'll loudly proclaim from stage, "My greatest fear is not having to work."

Cheese Strata

1/2 pound sausage
8 tablespoons butter
8 slices thin dry bread
8 ounces sharp cheddar cheese, grated
4 eggs, beaten
2-1/2 cups milk
1 tablespoon finely chopped onion
1-1/2 teaspoon salt
Dash of pepper
1 teaspoon prepared mustard

Brown and crumble sausage and drain off all fat. Butter bread slices and cut into cubes. Sprinkle grated cheese evenly on the bottom of a greased 9-by-9-inch baking dish. Top with sausage, followed by bread cubes. To the beaten eggs, add milk and remaining ingredients, mixing well. Pour mixture over the top of bread and let stand for at least a hour (best if left overnight).

Preheat oven to 350 degrees. Bake casserole for 45 minutes or until top becomes golden brown.

Serves 6

BUCK TRENT BREAKFAST THEATER
Highway 65 and 165
Hollister, MO 65672
(417) 335-5428
$$; no □; C; (4)

19

CAKES AND CREAMS DESSERT HOUSE

To set the mood for this unique establishment, you must first take yourself back to the glorious '50s. Your favorite hangout was the ice cream parlor within cruising distance of the high school. The inside was decorated in bright red and white, with a bubbling Wurlitzer jukebox in the corner stacked with the latest hits. You and your date would share a huge banana split and gaze starry-eyed at each other while the Everly Brothers serenaded you with their latest hit, "Dream."

When you step through the door of Cakes and Creams Dessert House, you'll feel like you took a quick trip back in time. But in addition to the jukebox and the cheery '50s decor, the owners have broadened the ice cream parlor concept by adding to the menu the most exquisite array of pies, cakes, and other desserts imaginable.

The pièce de résistance is the Cakes and Creams Supreme—a huge, freshly made funnel cake with a heaping scoop of your choice of ice cream, bathed in fresh strawberries, powdered sugar, and whipped cream. This decadent delight is topped with a miniature waffle cone and a perky red cherry. Besides being devilishly delicious, it's a feast for the eyes. Biting into a piece of chocolate, lemon, banana, or coconut cream pie, covered by gorgeous peaked meringue at least three inches high, becomes an adventure into ecstasy. The double-layered German chocolate cake is coated in a thick coconut and pecan frosting, so rich that even your better sense will encourage you to throw caution to the wind.

In all, the menu includes nineteen flavors of ice cream, eighteen assorted cream and fruit pies, fifteen different cakes, four cobblers, and over a hundred different flavor combinations of funnel cakes.

The creators of this alluring concept are John and Cristi Moore. In 1981 they decided to open an ice cream parlor on the strip, but wanting to offer customers more than their competition down the street, they hit upon the novel idea of a dessert parlor. In 1989 they hired a baker, Cindy Brooks, whose superb cake decorating talents have attracted national attention.

"It was quite an honor," says Cindy, referring to the cake she was asked to make to commemorate former President and Mrs. Bush's visit to Branson. "I put a detailed presidential seal on the top of the three-layer cake, which took me about five hours to recreate." The cake was received by tremendous acclamations, especially from the former first couple.

Cakes and Creams assures you "one of the sweetest times of your life." You'll know it's true when you take that first bite of one of their heavenly concoctions and feel that sweet smile of ecstasy cross your face.

Pumpkin Cheesecake

1 (8-ounce) package cream cheese,
  softened
1/3 cup sugar
1 teaspoon vanilla extract
1 cup sour cream
1 (8-ounce) container frozen
  whipped topping, thawed
1/2 cup canned pumpkin
1 teaspoon pumpkin pie spice
1 graham cracker pie crust

Beat cream cheese until smooth. Gradually beat in sugar and vanilla. When mixed, blend in sour cream. Fold in whipped topping, pumpkin, and pumpkin pie spice until thoroughly blended. Spoon into pie crust and chill for at least 4 hours.

Serves 6–8

CAKES AND CREAMS DESSERT HOUSE
2805 West Highway 76
Branson, MO 65616
(417) 334-4929
$; no □; C; (2)

THE CANDLESTICK INN

The Candlestick Inn sits on a ridge high atop Mt. Branson. Now if you think that "high atop" means that you're going to get the kind of view that you would from, say, Pike's Peak, you're mistaken. Instead, you'll take in a beautiful picture of Lake Taneycomo, downtown Branson, and the lush surrounding hills. This spot also offers one of the best fine-dining experiences in the area. Owner Mary Ann Bowman and Chef Andy Dirnberger have put together a menu that will entice you to stay in Branson a few extra days just to sample the cuisine.

One of the specialties here is the veal Oscar, tender meat paired with chunks of fresh crabmeat and asparagus topped with a creamy béarnaise sauce. Ordering the tournedos of beef summons up two succulent medallions served with a tomato crown and a rich Burgundy mushroom sauce. If you're in the mood for fish, try the Ozark traditional stuffed trout; caught fresh in Lake Taneycomo, it's filled with a delicious crabmeat dressing.

While the entrees are out of this world, be sure to save room for dessert. Sweet endings are one of Andy's hobbies and specialties, and no matter which you choose, you'll wish you had room for another.

Chef Andy Dirnberger came to The Candlestick Inn in 1988 with over twenty-five years of food-service experience in his hip pocket. The meals he prepares are not only delicious, but visual works of art as well.

The building itself originally was constructed as a private home in the early 1960s. By the end of the decade it had been turned into one of the few quality restaurants in the area. However, over the next few years its popularity declined, and the doors finally closed in the mid-seventies.

Mary Ann Bowman bought the restaurant in 1988 and immediately began making renovations. She installed thirty floor-to-ceiling windows that offer virtually every diner a breathtaking view, plus she enlarged the lounge and installed an authentic 1930s bar. Her biggest undertaking was the addition of a 1,200-square-foot deck that literally hangs over a sheer drop to the lake below.

The restaurant opens at 5 P.M., although the best time to go is at sunset so you can "ooh and ah" at one of the most beautiful sights the Ozarks has to offer. On the other hand, a visit here on a chilly overcast day is just as appealing, especially when a cheery fire is burning in the lounge fireplace.

Whenever you visit The Candlestick Inn you can always be assured of delicious food, fine service, and the best view that Mt. Branson has to offer.

Mt. Branson Rocky Road Cake

4 cups sugar
1 cup (2 sticks) margarine,
   softened
8 eggs
3 cups flour
1 teaspoon salt
8 tablespoons cocoa
2 teaspoons vanilla extract
1 cup nuts (your choice)
1 cup flaked coconut
1 jar marshmallow cream
Whipped cream and chocolate
   sauce to garnish (optional)

Preheat oven to 350 degrees. Cream sugar, margarine, and eggs. Mix flour, salt, and cocoa, and add to sugar mixture. Add vanilla, then fold in nuts and coconut. Pour batter into a 13-by-18-by-1-inch baking pan. Bake in oven for 30 to 40 minutes, then top with marshmallow cream. Pour **Rocky Road Frosting** over cake while still hot. Top with whipping cream and chocolate sauce if desired before serving.

Serves 10–12

Rocky Road Frosting

1 cup (2 sticks) margarine, melted
1 cup cocoa
1 cup half-and-half
2 (1-pound) boxes powdered sugar
1 tablespoon vanilla extract

Pour melted margarine into a bowl, and stir in cocoa and half-and-half. Whisk powdered sugar into mixture, followed by vanilla. Set aside until ready to use.

Makes 4–5 cups

THE CANDLESTICK INN
Mt. Branson
East Highway 76
Branson, MO 65616
(417) 334-3633
Reservations recommended
$–$$$; □; C–D; (1)

CHEF RICHARD'S LONG CREEK CAFE

Branson's Table Rock Lake is a serpentine body of water with numerous hidden tributaries waiting to be explored. One of the treasures that you'll discover hidden in a bend of Long Creek is Chef Richard's cafe. The restaurant is small and the hours are erratic, but the food and service are among the best in the area.

Proprietor Richard Groves is a graduate of Johnson and Wales Culinary Arts College and a member of the American Culinary Association. This is not to imply that the bill of fare belongs in a foreign language course; the mainstay of the restaurant is Ozark-style cooking with a few Italian delicacies added for variety.

Richard loves seafood, and his shrimp scampi bears this out. Prepared with a subtle blend of garlic butter, white wine, lemon juice, and a few secrets Richard won't divulge, it is melt-in-your-mouth delicious. The seasoning for his blackened mako shark has a bite to it that would make the shark envious. His charbroiled chicken breast, topped with a spicy tomato basil sauce, could be meal in itself without the salad, homemade soup, baked potato, and homemade bread that accompanies it (and every entree). As for his country-cooking specialties, just try the deep-fried whole catfish served with a heaping mound of homemade tartar sauce.

Richard was introduced to cooking by his grandmother at a very early age. His grandfather had been a highly esteemed chef in St. Louis during the Depression and was one of the few chefs in the area that maintained his job. "I guess cooking is in my blood," says Richard, "although I knew nothing about my grandfather's background until just a few years ago."

Richard was one of the main bakers at College of the Ozarks and taught baking at the college for four years. "I really enjoyed baking," he says, "but I knew that to accomplish what I wanted, I needed a cooking degree. That's when I decided to enroll at Johnson and Wales." The decision paid off, and he became head chef at several country clubs along the East Coast. He returned to Branson in 1991 and opened Chef Richard's the following year.

The restaurant is a part of Gage's Long Creek Lodge, a no-frills motel that caters to fishermen and budget-conscious vacationers. Hosts Carl and Jeanne Gage also own an antique store in Hollister, and the overflow from the store decorates the restaurant. Gorgeous antique stained-glass lamps illuminate each dining table. A 1937 working jukebox sits in one corner, and an antique hammered-copper cappuccino maker resides in another. The assorted knickknacks perched precariously on shelves are reminiscent of a great-grandmother who hated to part with her treasures.

Chef Richard's Long Creek Cafe evokes an interesting blend of yesterday and today. A delightful experience for those willing to seek it out.

24

Chicken Milanaise

4 boneless, skinless chicken breast
  halves
1 egg
2 cups flour
1 teaspoon white pepper, plus
  additional to taste
Salt and garlic powder to taste
3 cups bread crumbs
1/2 cup grated Parmesan cheese
1 tablespoon butter
Parsley sprigs to garnish

Whisk egg until foamy, then set aside. In a separate bowl, combine flour, 1 teaspoon white pepper, salt, and garlic powder, and set aside. In a third bowl mix together bread crumbs and Parmesan cheese, and set aside. Dip chicken breasts in egg wash, then flour mixture, and finally bread crumbs. Melt butter in a skillet and add prepared chicken breasts. Cook for 4 minutes on each side or until firm. Transfer to dinner plates and top with *Lime Butter Sauce*. Garnish with parsley and serve.

Serves 2–4

Lime Butter Sauce

1 small shallot, chopped
1/4 cup dry white wine
Juice of 4 limes
1 cup (2 sticks) lightly salted
  butter, melted

Combine shallots, lime juice, white wine, and butter. Mix well and set aside.

Makes about 1-1/2 cups

CHEF RICHARD'S LONG CREEK CAFE
Highway 86 to Lake Road 86-26
Ridgedale, MO 65739
(417) 335-6055
$–$$; □; C; (11)

CONFETTI'S RESTAURANT

When owner Bob Sarver was choosing a name for his new restaurant, he looked for one that would represent a fun, party atmosphere and hit upon "Confetti's." Balloons and streamers decorate the pink menus, adding an extra festive touch. Though the atmosphere is lighthearted, Confetti's serves some seriously good food. "All of our sauces are made from scratch," Bob says proudly. "Nothing comes out of a can. I even use Louisiana white lump crabmeat in all my crab dishes. It's the best you can buy."

Although a wide variety appears on the menu, Bob feels like his Italian fare is the best. The sauce on the spaghetti Bolognese, for example, simmers for over six hours and contains choice Italian sausage and ground sirloin. No shortcuts mar the lasagna either; Bob uses real ricotta cheese and slowly bakes the dish to capture all the flavor.

"It's taken a while for our food to catch on because we offer a different type of menu," says Bob. "Take our hamburgers for example. We don't serve them the traditional way, with lettuce, tomato, and onions. Ours are topped with hollandaise sauce, sour cream and blue cheese or Swiss cheese, and mushrooms." Once you've tried one, you'll be back for another.

Bob loves to experiment with different foods. Most of the dishes on Confetti's menu come from recipes that he has taken and enhanced with his own special touch. He spent the last twenty-eight years in the food business learning how to cook from professional chefs that "didn't mind sharing their secrets."

Andy Bray, owner of the Wooden Nickel, was responsible for bringing Bob to Branson. "We met when we were both working on the corporate level for a nationally known restaurant chain," Bob recalls. "After Andy moved to Branson, he tried to get me to visit for several years, but I liked living in Houston. Besides, I thought, what in the world is there for me in Branson, Missouri?" Bob finally came for a visit in 1990 and fell in love with the area. He and his family made the move in 1991, and in February 1992 he opened Confetti's.

In addition to being a popular restaurant, Confetti's has become one of the hottest rock-and-roll nightclubs in Branson. You'll often see members of Mickey Gilley's and Moe Bandy's band there after their evening performances.

Located on West Highway 76 in the Holiday Inn, Confetti's is open for breakfast, lunch, and dinner. Any item you choose to eat will give you cause for a celebration.

Crab St. James

1 pound white lump crabmeat
1 bay leaf
1/4 pound fresh mushrooms, diced
1/2 cup diced red bell pepper
1/4 cup diced green bell pepper
1/2 white onion, diced
1 cup (2 sticks) butter
1/2 cup Chablis wine
8 prepared crêpes
Chopped parsley to garnish

In a skillet or large sauté pan, sauté bay leaf and vegetables in butter until tender but still firm. Add crabmeat and simmer for 3 minutes. Add wine and simmer for an additional 5 minutes. Remove from heat and strain off liquid. Place 4 to 5 heaping tablespoons of mixture in the center of each crêpe and fold. Place 2 crêpes in each of 4 small casseroles or rarebit dishes and microwave on high for 45 seconds. Top each with *Hollandaise Sauce* and chopped parsley.

Serves 4

Hollandaise Sauce

10 egg yolks
1/4 cup lemon juice
2 cups (4 sticks) butter
Dash of Tabasco sauce

In a mixing bowl, add lemon juice to egg yolks and blend. Set aside. Melt butter slowly over low heat in saucepan, and do not let brown. Remove from heat.

Place mixing bowl containing egg mixture in a boiling water bath. Blending with a wire whisk, cook until thickened (do not let eggs scramble). Slowly add melted butter, blending with the wire whisk. Remove from heat. Stir before pouring over crêpes.

Makes about 2 cups

CONFETTI'S RESTAURANT
1420 West Highway 76
Branson, MO 65616
(417) 334-5101
$–$$; □; C; (2)

27

DEVIL'S POOL RESTAURANT

In the early 1920s, Frisco Railroad tycoon Harry Worman purchased 160 acres of virgin land in the Ozark Mountains south of Branson. Here he built a beautiful Tudor-style home encircled by huge cedar trees, large servants' quarters, and a stable. When two of his close friends died, Worman took it upon himself to care for their only child, Dorothy, some forty-odd years his junior. As was the custom, he married her and brought her to live at Big Cedar, his remote estate.

Lonesome and secluded, Dorothy ran away with the caretaker to Mexico, where she reportedly died a mysterious death. Harry cremated her body and brought her ashes back to the estate, where he scattered them over his property.

Dorothy's death is just one of the mysteries surrounding Big Cedar Resort. One thing is certain, however; when you visit here, you will be awed by the overwhelming beauty. A clear mountain stream cascades down three tiers of the beautifully landscaped property. The rambling, multistoried lodge sits high on the hillside, offering a breathtaking view of the lake below.

Resort amenities include horseback riding, a private boat dock, and shuttle service to one of the finest and most picturesque restaurants in the area, Devil's Pool. Resembling a mountain lodge, mounted wild game covers the restaurant's walls. The expression on a large moose head crowned with huge antlers actually looks happy, probably because of the delicious aromas coming from the kitchen.

The cooking staff here excels in tried-and-true standards. Hillbilly Meatloaf is a special blend of ground beef and pork with just the right touch of seasoning. The Walleye Provençal is a moist white fish, pan-fried and topped with tomato, lemon, garlic, and butter. Smoked on the premises, the country ham steak guarantees twelve ounces of pure enjoyment. Other offerings include a tasty catfish, country-fried steak, and the always popular prime rib. For dessert, there is nothing better than the chocolate cake bathed in luscious candied cherries.

The breakfast and luncheon buffet serves up made-to-order omelets and Belgian waffles. Carved meats, homemade cobblers, and a varied selection of beef, poultry, and pasta also appear at lunch.

The masterhand behind the scene is kitchen manager Dyan Kennedy, a petite young woman with giant cooking talents. Dyan is a Chicago transplant who claims she learned to cook in the school of hard knocks. When the restaurant first opened in 1989, Dyan did all the cooking. Today she supervises a staff of thirty-six who at times serve 1,350 people a day.

Although Big Cedar Resort may be cloaked in mystery, there's no mystery why Devil's Pool has become one of the most frequented restaurants in the Ozarks.

Stuffed Ozark Catfish

10 (4–5-ounce) catfish fillets
1/2 pound crabmeat
1/2 pound shrimp, peeled, deveined, and chopped
1 cup finely chopped celery
1/2 cup finely chopped white onion
1/2 cup dry white wine
1 teaspoon crushed bay leaves
1 teaspoon crushed oregano
1 teaspoon thyme
1/2 cup (1 stick) butter, melted, plus addition for basting
Salt, white pepper, and cayenne pepper to taste
2 eggs, beaten
1 loaf bread, crumbled

Preheat oven to 350 degrees. In a large bowl, combine crabmeat, shrimp, celery, onion, white wine, bay leaves, oregano, thyme, butter, salt, and peppers. Mix well and set aside.

In a second bowl, mix together eggs and bread crumbs until thoroughly moistened. Combine mixtures and mix well. Wash fillets and place 5 on an oiled baking sheet. Spoon stuffing onto the middle of each fillet (do not spoon any stuffing on the ends). Make a slit down the middle of remaining fillets (do not cut through to the ends). Place cut fillets over the others, allowing stuffing to show through. Baste each with butter and bake for 15 to 20 minutes until fish is firm. Serve with rice or home-style potatoes.

Serves 4–5

DEVIL'S POOL RESTAURANT
Big Cedar Lodge
612 Devil's Pool Road
Ridgedale, MO 65739
(417) 335-5141
Reservations recommended
$-$$$; □; C; (11)

"The building we're in now is like a barn compared to our old restaurant," says Dimitrios Tsahiridis, owner of Dimitri's. The "barn" he refers to is an intimate dining room cloaked in yards of gathered damask. Subsequent to a fire in February 1992, Dimitri's temporary headquarters has become the Roark Motel, but his new restaurant will open for business soon.

A rendering of the new restaurant is displayed in the main dining room. When completed, it will stand out as one of Branson's most unusual establishments. Fashioned in a Greek architectural style complete with columns, the structure will float on Lake Taneycomo.

"The new restaurant will have two dining rooms," says Dimitri. "One will offer gourmet dining and the other will cater to families. In addition, I am going to put in a piano bar and an European pastry shop." The restaurateur's signature blue-and-white color scheme will enhance the new location as well.

Dimitri is truly an American success story. One of eight children, he grew up on a farm in northern Greece. ("Where Alexander the Great was from," he is quick to add.) At nineteen his family moved to St. Louis, where he worked as a busboy in a local restaurant and learned the business from the ground up. He married into a family of restaurateurs, and his father-in-law convinced him to come to Branson. Dimitri recalls, "When I moved here in 1976, there were a lot of greasy spoons and coffee shops. I managed a local restaurant for eight months and then decided to open my own."

Dimitri's is anything but a "greasy spoon." The menu tempts diners with both Greek and American delicacies—tender leg of lamb, pan-fried abalone steaks, duck à l'orange, and steak Diane. When the waiter rolls the dessert cart to your table, you'll have difficulty deciding among the delectable tortes and exotic cakes. (The secret is to invite several friends with you and sample theirs!)

Regardless of where Dimitri is located when you take in Branson, find him and sample some of his delicious cuisine.

Dimitri's Revani Semolina Cake

1/2 cup flour
1/2 teaspoon baking powder
1-1/3 cups fine semolina or farina
(cream of wheat)
4 large eggs, separated
1/2 cup sugar
1/2 cup olive oil
Finely grated zest of 2 lemons
1/2 teaspoon almond extract
1/2 cup orange juice
1 teaspoon vinegar
A pinch of cream of tartar
1/2 cup blanched, slivered
almonds

Preheat oven to 350 degrees. Line a 10-by-10-by-3-inch cake pan with baking parchment. Sift together flour and baking powder, then stir in semolina. Beat egg yolks, sugar, olive oil, lemon zest, and almond extract together until pale and creamy. Beat in flour mixture, splashing with orange juice to moisten.

Moisten a cloth with vinegar and use to wipe the inside of a mixing bowl. Place egg whites in the bowl and beat with cream of tartar until stiff peaks form. Fold into batter, pour into prepared pan, and sprinkle top with almonds. Bake for approximately 45 minutes until cake becomes golden brown. Remove from oven and, while still hot, cut into 2-1/2-inch squares. Slowly pour **Chilled Syrup** over all and serve.

Serves 12–16

Chilled Syrup

3/4 cup sugar
Zest and juice of 2 lemons
1/4 teaspoon almond extract
1-1/2 cups water

One day ahead, combine sugar, lemon zest, lemon juice, and water in a saucepan. Bring to a boil and simmer for 5 minutes. Add almond extract and stir. Remove from heat and chill overnight.

Makes about 2-1/2 cups

DIMITRI'S
Call for location
(417) 334-0888
Reservations recommended
$$–$$$; □; C–D; (1)

31

DONOVAN'S HILLBILLY INN RESTAURANT

The front door to Donovan's Hillbilly Inn Restaurant, a quaint log cabin–style structure, sits not more than ten steps from West Highway 76. A discernible aroma of hickory and sassafras emanating from the meat smoker out back immediately engulfs anyone who approaches.

Just inside the front door an open-view refrigerator displays a mouthwatering assortment of ham, sausage, brisket, turkey, and thick slabs of bacon, all fresh from the smoker. The bacon will eventually be served in the restaurant, but the hams and turkeys are for sale. Many have become the main course for lavish parties in the area.

The restaurant is advertised as having the best breakfast in Branson, and it definitely ranks in the top ten. The specialty here is a whole center-cut ham steak with red eye gravy and "fixins"—fried potatoes, a big bowl of grits, fried apples, sausage gravy, two fresh eggs, buttermilk biscuits, juice, and coffee. After tackling a "Hillbilly Inn World Famous Breakfast," you're usually too full to jump right up and leave. So, the management has thoughtfully provided an exquisite southern view of the Ozarks to enjoy while your food digests.

The establishment is run by native Missourians Frank and Vivian Donovan. Frank opened his first restaurant, The Streetcar Grill, in 1948. "I ran the restaurant," says Frank, "but I didn't really know how to cook. One day my chef walked out and I had to take over. Let me tell you, I learned how to cook quick!"

Frank also spent ten years as head of Greyhound's food and beverage division, traveling a twelve-state area. As he recalls, "After ten years of being constantly on the road and eating terminal restaurant food (no pun intended), I decided it was time to take it a little easier. We decided to retire in Branson and I opened up this restaurant."

Today most of the cooking is done by Rick Cofer, a Louisiana Cajun who has been with Frank since 1984. Rick handles smoking the meats and baking the scrumptious desserts. His personal favorite is the pecan pie, but his strawberry pie topped with whipped cream is a treat no one should leave Branson without trying.

The Hillbilly Inn Restaurant gets a lot of repeat business from year to year, and Frank seems to remember everyone. Although he'll stop and spend a few moments with you, it's not unusual to hear him stop abruptly with a "Gotta get cuttin' bacon. See you later."

Hillbilly Inn Pecan Pie

8 eggs
2 cups light corn syrup
1 cup sugar
1 cup firmly packed brown sugar
4 tablespoons butter
2 tablespoons vanilla extract
1/4 teaspoon salt
2 cups pecan halves
2 (9-inch) deep-dish pie crusts,
   uncooked and thawed

Preheat oven to 350 degrees. Break eggs into a large bowl and beat well. Stir in remaining ingredients except pecans. When ingredients are thoroughly combined, add pecans and mix well. Pour filling into pie crusts. Place on middle oven rack and bake for 1 hour or until pecans turn a dark golden brown.

Serves 12–16

DONOVAN'S HILLBILLY INN RESTAURANT
1166 West Highway 76
Branson, MO 65616
(417) 334-6644
$–$$; □; C; (2)

33

DUCK CAFE

During Branson's tourist season, people arrive from far and wide in a vast array of vehicles. But undoubtedly the strangest one you'll come across on Highway 76 is an amphibious carrier called a "duck." If you follow this "duck" home, you'll run head long into one of the busiest, most bustling restaurants in Branson, the Duck Cafe.

Open for breakfast, lunch, and dinner, Duck Cafe caters to the throng waiting to ride the ducks. The menu items are designed to serve a huge turnover of guests, yet the restaurant maintains a high quality standard. The fanciest thing on the menu is a twelve-ounce rib-eye steak, but it's tender and cooked to your liking. A huge selection of sandwiches beckons, each fresh and delicious (the club is one of the best in town). The homemade chili contains huge chunks of ground beef swimming in a spicy sauce.

A buffet is offered at each meal and the breakfast selections are especially delightful. A real egg dip covers the thick French toast, and a hot syrup accompanies the light pancakes. The eggs are freshly scrambled and the blueberry muffins homemade. A large variety of seasonal fresh fruit always graces the spread.

"Ride the Ducks" is one of Branson's most popular attractions, and the fleet of twenty-one vessels transports over 500 people per hour on a spectacular seventy-minute tour, including a big splash into Table Rock Lake. Passengers have a chance to pilot during the tour, and each one receives a captain's certificate at the end of the trip.

The ducks are part of owner Bob McDowell's collection of World War II memorabilia. An avid collector, Bob has decorated the walls of the restaurant with his smaller treasures, and he includes his larger finds on the tour. Within a beautiful hillside compound, tour-goers can see an amphibious Studebaker "Weasel" designed for over-snow operations, a "mechanical mule," and many one-of-a-kind vehicles, all remnants from past wars.

If you're undecided whether to ride a duck or just watch them "fly" by, the Duck Cafe is the perfect place to decide. It's much more comfortable than a duck blind and you don't have to quack to get attention.

(*Author's* note: Some changes were being discussed at press time regarding the extent of food services that would continue here. Call ahead for information.)

Bread Pudding

1 cup (2 sticks) margarine
5-1/2 cups bread crumbs
5 eggs
2-1/2 cups sugar
1-1/2 quarts milk
2 teaspoons vanilla extract
2 teaspoons cinnamon
1/2 teaspoon nutmeg

Preheat oven to 350 degrees. Melt margarine and set aside. In a second bowl, finely crush bread crumbs and set aside. In a large mixing bowl, beat eggs until fluffy. With mixer set on high, slowly add 2 cups sugar. Reduce speed and add milk and vanilla. Pour margarine into a 9-by-13-inch cake pan and distribute evenly around bottom and sides. Add bread crumbs and spread evenly over bottom of pan. Do not stir. Sprinkle top of crumbs with remaining 1/2 cup sugar, cinnamon, and nutmeg. Place on middle rack of oven and bake for 45 minutes or until pudding rises and cracks around the top.

Serves 10–12

DUCK CAFE
2320 West Highway 76
Branson, MO 65616
(417) 335-5350
$; □; C; (2)

If you like down-home entertainment while you're dining, then Fall Creek Steak House is the place to go. However, don't bother with fancy dancing shoes; instead, bring a catcher's mitt or a hot pad. You'll need it when they "throw the rolls."

When Jan and Jim Gibbs opened their restaurant, they looked for something in addition to great steaks to offer their customers and hit upon the idea of roll throwing. If you want a hot homemade roll, just holler at one of the two professional throwers, who'll toss you one from wherever they happen to be standing. Besides the flying bread, Fall Creek Steak House serves up a big bottomless bowl of salad with every one of the numerous entree selections.

Steaks cooked over an open hickory log fire are the house specialty, but the Gibbs Ribs, cooked long and slow and coated with a special barbecue sauce, taste delectable as well. The menu also features several chicken selections, including the tasty Apple-Glazed Chicken Breast. If you're looking for something on the lighter side, try the Mountain Grown Vegetable Beef Soup. No ordinary stew meat in this; it's made with hefty chunks of steak.

The restaurant, located on Fall Creek Road, is quite easy to find. Just look for the enormous plaster steer in the parking lot. Behind the steer stands a building constructed of barn siding, reminiscent of a ranch house from an old cowboy movie. However, few cowboys would take the time to hang huge Boston ferns on the front porch or build a fan-cooled dining deck overlooking scenic Fall Creek.

Jan and Jack are no strangers to the restaurant business. As Jan puts it, "We've owned umpteen." They moved to Jackson, Mississippi, in the '60s to open an insurance company, but instead founded a chain of pizzerias. They've owned several restaurants in Branson, but a steak house was Jim's dream. The fantasy became reality in September 1992, when Fall Creek Steak House opened. Now you'll see Jim behind the grill cooking almost every night and having the time of his life. "We've gotten most of our family involved in our business," Jan says. "Our daughter Lisa does the zillion things I don't have time to do and our son-in-law manages the other restaurant we own."

Whether you're looking for a good meal or just want to practice some good old-fashioned roll throwing, try Fall Creek Steak House.

Apple-Glazed Chicken Breasts

4 (6–8-ounce) boneless, skinless
    chicken breasts
1 cup apple juice
1/2 cup honey

Mix apple juice and honey together until a thin glaze forms. Separate mixture into 2 equal portions. Keep second half of the glaze warm for use when serving. Grill chicken breasts over charcoal or hickory wood until firm. Using half the glaze as a baste, coat chicken about 5 minutes before removing it from the grill. When chicken is done, dip each breast into the second half of the glaze and serve.

Serves 4

FALL CREEK STEAK HOUSE
Highway 165 and Fall Creek Road
Branson, MO 65616
(417) 336-5060
$–$$; □; C; (4)

37

GARCIA'S RESTAURANT

When Ray and Connie Garcia opened their restaurant on Highway 76 in 1971, the only buildings that stood between them and downtown Branson were a couple of hotels and a smattering of houses. Today, they are surrounded by motels, gift shops, theaters, and numerous other "strip" attractions that seem to stretch on for miles.

The building they currently operate in was one of those original "smattering of houses"—a tiny white stucco hacienda with a big bright red welcoming canopy over the front door. The restaurant only seats eighty, but those waiting to get into Garcia's during the season know it's well worth the wait.

The menu consists of traditional Mexican food offerings, but you haven't had real Mexican food until you sample Connie and Ray's. Every item served is made from scratch; there's not a prepackaged tortilla or tamale in the place.

The chili con carne dishes up a savory blend of exotic spices in a rich sauce with enormous chunks of lean pork loin in every spoonful. The cheese enchiladas are enticing in looks as well as in flavor. A delicate blend of longhorn colby and Monterey Jack cheeses rolled in a light flour tortilla, the taste is out of this world (especially when topped with lots of the homemade hot sauce). Connie's tamales combine pork and chicken in a thick dough. She even cuts and cleans the corn husks that they're wrapped in. One of Ray and Connie's specialties is *menudo*, a thick Mexican stew with tripe as its main ingredient. Although pungent in taste and aroma, Connie serves it with oregano, lemon juice, and crushed red pepper, which helps to diminish the discernible flavor of the tripe.

Ray was born in Salmanca, Mexico, but moved to Kansas City at such an early age he considers himself a native Missourian. In 1948 his family opened the first Mexican restaurant in Kansas City, called Las Palmas. He later forged out on his own and opened four Garcia's. "We had a good business," says Ray, "but I decided I wanted to raise my kids in a better environment. After all, in the long run what else do I have except my kids? When I told Connie we were moving to Branson, she cried. Now you can't get her out of here."

Connie is a twinkling brown-eyed beauty from Mexico City who had never lived in the States before she married Ray. "I knew he had a restaurant, but I thought it was just a sideline to his jewelry store. I didn't even know how to cook when I moved here," she laughs, "but Ray and his family soon had me in the kitchen cooking right along with them." Today Connie is still in the kitchen cooking, and her talents are unsurpassed.

Eating at Garcia's is a truly enjoyable experience even if you don't speak a word of Spanish. However, don't be surprised if, at the end of the meal, you begin shouting "olé!"

Guacamole Salad

3 large ripe avocados
2 medium tomatoes, diced
1 teaspoon diced onion
1/2 teaspoon lemon juice
1 jalapeño pepper, diced very fine
5 or 6 sprigs cilantro, diced
   (optional)
Salt to taste

Peel avocados and remove pit. Place avocados in a large bowl and mash into a paste-like consistency. Add tomatoes, onions, and lemon juice. Add jalapeño peppers little by little until desired spiciness is reached. Add cilantro and salt to taste. Serve over chopped lettuce as a salad or with chips as a dip.

Serves 6–8

GARCIA'S RESTAURANT
3016 West Highway 76
Branson, MO 65616
(417) 334-5801
$; □; C; (2)

There's nothing fancy about The Hungry Hunter, and the decor is what you might find at any roadside cafe. Comfy booths line one wall, and plain tables and chairs are situated about the room. A few deer heads and mounted crappies, remnants of the previous owner's honeymoon, adorn the walls. However, don't let the austerity dissuade you from sitting down and taking a minute to study the menu. You'll be delighted and overwhelmed with the selections offered.

Breakfast is served anytime, and anytime is perfect for sampling the huge biscuits here, a meal in themselves. One biscuit covers a whole plate and, when smothered in thick sausage gravy, will tide you over until lunch. The Mexican omelet is loaded with chunks of garden vegetables and topped with cheese and salsa.

After tasting the fried chicken, the lunch and dinner specialty, you'll know why the menu states, "You'll crow about it!" Hungry Hunter offers a wide variety of sandwiches and steaks, including Bob's Special Smothered Steak, an appetizing concoction of peppers, onions, tomatoes, melted cheese, and mounds of sour cream.

Bob Berthelson, who bills himself not only as owner but chief cook and bottle washer, too, entered the restaurant business literally through the back door. He owned a motel in Kansas City and leased out the adjoining restaurant. "One day the people leasing the restaurant walked out the front door and I walked in the back to the kitchen and started cooking. I had no idea what I was doing and I hated it."

Over the years and through fourteen restaurants, Bob began to enjoy cooking, and most mornings find him in The Hungry Hunter kitchen making biscuits and tossing omelets. Although his breakfasts are delicious and his homemade chili out of this world, Bob's true talent lies in baking. "I had an old cook at one of the restaurants I owned who made the best pies. Late at night, he'd be in the kitchen concocting something or other and I'd stand there and watch him, fascinated. Before I knew it, he had me in there experimenting with various recipes and coming up with my own creations." One of Bob's favorites is a creamy peanut butter pie, but he admits he has a hard time resisting his sour cream raisin. "And not a calorie in the whole thing," Bob will say with a wink.

Whether you happen into The Hungry Hunter for breakfast, lunch, or dinner, if there are lots of cars parked outside, you'll know that Bob's cooking.

Sour Cream Raisin Pie

3 cups milk
3 egg yolks
3 tablespoons cornstarch
2 cups sugar
1 pat butter
Dash of salt
1 tablespoon vanilla extract
1 cup sour cream
1 cup raisins
2 (9-inch) prebaked pie crusts
Whipped cream to garnish

In a large saucepan, over medium heat, combine milk, eggs, cornstarch, sugar, butter, and salt. Bring to a boil, stirring constantly, and add vanilla, sour cream, and raisins. Mix well and pour into a prepared pie crusts. Chill and top with whipped cream before serving.

Serves 12–16

THE HUNGRY HUNTER
Highway 13
Reeds Spring, MO 65737
(417) 272-8680
$–$$; no □; C; (8)

"I am a devout collector of everything," says Mary Jane Bolt, owner of Mary Jane's. "When I opened this place I furnished it with furniture and other things that I had collected over the years and had stored in my garage. But even after I finished decorating the restaurant, my garage still looked full."

Mary Jane's indeed presents an eclectic but tasteful assortment of furniture and odds and ends. Antique sideboards and hutches stand in the three small dining rooms, and flea market finds adorn the walls and china cabinets. Meals appear on her mother's and grandmother's china much to the delight of the guests.

Even the curtains and tablecloths reflect Mary Jane's individual style. One week you may see crisp pink rosebud–patterned swags hanging over the windows. The next week, she will have transformed the curtains into table coverings and napkins.

The only thing that ever remains the same here is the delicious food. Mary Jane's menu, written on chalkboards, consists of a variety of light delicacies. The garden vegetable quiche is fluffy and brimming with fresh produce. The crab salad and chicken salad both contain huge chunks of meat in a creamy mayonnaise dressing. The broccoli soufflé and vegetable strata are pure ambrosia. Her daily specials vary but often include baked chicken over garden rice or a delicious seafood fettuccine. Desserts include a scrumptious baked fudge and a mouth-watering peach Melba topped with raspberries and fresh cream.

Mary Jane and her husband moved to the area from Chicago, where they had lived in the same house for twenty-seven years. Her brother-in-law, a regular Branson vacationer for many years, kept raving about the place and finally convinced the couple to check it out. "We immediately fell in love with Branson and decided to move here. That was ten years ago," says Mary Jane. "Since then, my brother-in-law has never been back even for a visit."

She first opened a tea room on the strip. Later some friends discovered the cozy little house on Highway 13 that she's in now, so she closed the tea room and opened Mary Jane's. "This old house is more in keeping with my style of food and decorating," she adds.

Mary Jane's is only open from 11 A.M. to 3 P.M., Monday through Saturday. Seating is limited to fifty, and the place is always crowded. If there's a wait when you arrive, take the opportunity to visit the unique gift shop next door. Or, sit under one of the big shade trees in the front yard and prepare your taste buds for one of the most inviting meals in the area.

Strawberry Soup

1 (15-ounce) package frozen
strawberries, thawed (reserve
juice)
2 cups sour cream
2-1/2 tablespoons vanilla extract
6 tablespoons powdered sugar
2 tablespoons grenadine
1/4 cup half-and-half

Whirl strawberries and sour cream in a blender on slow speed until mixed well. Add vanilla, sugar, and grenadine, and mix until smooth. Add half-and-half and mix again until blended. Chill. Shake well before serving. (Note: For a delicious alternative to the strawberries, substitute fresh or frozen peaches and a dash of cinnamon, canned purple plums, or other favorite fruits in same quantity as above.)

Serves 6

MARY JANE'S
Highway 13 North
Branson West, MO 65737
(417) 272-8908
$; no □; C; (9)

43

MEL'S RESTAURANT

As you enter Branson from the north on Highway 65, one of the very first things to catch your eye is a gigantic picture of country music super-entertainer Mel Tillis. On the hill behind the picture sits his restaurant, appropriately enough called Mel's.

While Mel himself is quite an accomplished cook (his seafood gumbo would knock your socks off), you won't find him performing in the kitchen. More than likely, he'll be appearing on stage next door in his beautiful 2,101-seat theater. Although Mel and his wife Judy take an active interest in the restaurant, the actual running of it is left in the very capable hands of Giaco and Janet Broccli. The Brocclis divide their time between Branson and Mystic, Connecticut, where they own another restaurant, The Ship's Lantern.

In daily residence is general manager Michael Cleary, who does a superb job of running the restaurant, taking care of customers, and catering to the needs of guest celebrities performing at Mel's theater. "When Debbie Reynolds was here," Michael recalls, "she would call me and say, 'Michael, can I have some Cheerios and a spoon? I promise to bring it back.'"

The menu at Mel's offers a wide variety of tempting food, and the steaks are some of the juiciest you've ever eaten, but Michael unabashedly claims that their breakfast, lunch, and dinner buffets are the best in Branson. Indeed, with offerings like the tender beef bourguignon and succulent baked chicken, the noon and evening buffet come off as anything but run-of-the-mill. The chicken potpie is loaded with tender white meat and scads of tasty vegetables. The lavish spread also offers nine varieties of salad, which may include a delicious mustard potato salad or fresh cucumbers and tomatoes in a marvelous vinaigrette. The buffet will often feature ethnic foods from south of the border and Italy.

After dinner you'll want to visit the Mole Hole Ballroom (named so because Mel likes moles), located below the restaurant, to enjoy live music and dancing seven nights a week. As a matter of fact, many well-known celebrities like Merle Haggard, Charlie Pride, Barbara Fairchild, and even Mel himself often pop in after the 8 P.M. show for a jam session. If you harbor a desire to sing on a Branson stage yourself, visit the Mole Hole on Monday nights during the Gong Show.

There are a multitude of great reasons to visit Branson. If one of yours is to see Mel Tillis perform, why not eat at his restaurant, too!

Chicken Fiesta

8 boneless, skinless chicken breast
 halves
1 pound linguine, cooked
1 cup chopped onion
1 cup chopped green bell pepper
1/2 cup olive oil
2 cups chopped tomatoes
2 cups salsa
2 cups shredded sharp cheddar
 cheese
2 cups sliced, pitted jumbo black
 olives
1 cup chopped green onions

Grill or broil chicken breasts for 2 minutes, then set aside.

In a large pan, sauté onions and peppers in olive oil over medium heat for 4 minutes. Add chicken, tomatoes, and salsa, and simmer for 3 minutes. Reheat pasta by placing in boiling water for 10 seconds. Drain well and place on a warmed serving platter. Spoon chicken mixture over pasta and top with cheddar cheese, black olives, and green onions. Serve with a green salad and breadsticks.

Serves 4–6

MEL'S RESTAURANT
Highway 248 and 65
Branson, MO 65616
(417) 335-5410
$–$$; □; C; (1)

THE OLD APPLE MILL RESTAURANT

The Old Apple Mill Restaurant sits just off West Highway 76 in a cluster of trees behind the Hall of Fame Motor Inn. Diners enter the cozy wooden structure through an inviting bright red door, flanked by two brass coach lanterns.

The interior typifies what you'd expect to find inside an old mill—a vaulted ceiling, exposed rafters, wooden floors, and lots of windows, allowing for an abundance of cheery sunlight. An antique buggy with original velvet upholstery stands in a prominent setting. An exquisite, leaded stained-glass window, which once graced the wall of a church, hangs over the register. The wallpaper displays a subtle pattern of peaches and grapes, and homey country curtains adorn the windows.

The design and decor of the restaurant was the brainchild of owners Chris and Lori Lucchi. "We were leasing a restaurant when Chris suggested that we build one of our own," recalls Lori. "One night he sketched out this floor plan on a brown paper sack, and before we knew it, we were opened for business. The most fun was scouring flea markets and antique stores for the decor."

The varied menu items stay in keeping with the restaurant's theme. Perhaps the most popular is the "Ultimate Feast," commencing with a large platter of succulent prime rib, marinated and grilled chicken, and an exquisite seafood Mornay. The meal is complemented by freshly baked bread, apple muffins, and cinnamon rolls, a large bowl of fresh salad, mashed potatoes and gravy, corn on the cob, and ham and beans. Be sure you're hungry if you order this spread, because the Lucchis don't skimp on portions.

If a "feast" is not quite what you had in mind, try one of the many delicious entrees. The stuffed red snapper, filled with tasty crabmeat and smothered in a creamy crab sauce, is pure ecstasy. The smoked trout, slow cooked over hickory wood, puts a new twist on a favorite fish. Another smoked delicacy is the turkey breast, and you'd have to beat the bushes to find one any better.

Chris began his career in the food industry at the tender age of fifteen, when he was hired as a cook for a Chinese restaurant. He met Lori when she came to work for him in a Springfield restaurant he was managing. "I didn't know much about this business at that time," she says. "My biggest claim to fame was being the most popular kid at show-and-tell because my father, who worked for Boeing inspecting Minuteman missiles, supplied me with all sorts of neat stuff."

Today, Lori and Chris's popularity stems not only from the "neat stuff" they serve in their restaurant but also from their convenient proximity to most of the theaters. So, if you're going to a show, start off at The Old Apple Mill. It will be the beginning of an evening you'll never forget.

Seafood Mornay

16 scallops, cleaned
16 shrimp, peeled and deveined
4 ounces snow crab meat
8 large mushrooms, sliced
Salt and pepper to taste
1 tablespoon butter

Preheat oven to 400 degrees. In a sauté pan or skillet, sauté seafood and mushrooms in butter and season to taste. Pour mixture into a casserole dish and top with **Mornay Sauce**. Heat in oven until sauce begins to bubble, about 15 minutes.

Serves 4

Mornay Sauce

1 tablespoon minced shallots
2 cups half-and-half
1/4 teaspoon granulated garlic
1/2 teaspoon basil
1/4 teaspoon oregano
1/4 teaspoon white pepper
1/4 teaspoon salt
2 tablespoons dry white wine
1/2 cup grated Monterey Jack
   cheese
1/4 cup grated Gruyère cheese
1/4 cup grated Parmesan cheese
1/4 cup flour
3 tablespoons butter, softened

Sauté shallots in a sauté pan or skillet. Over low heat, add half-and-half and remaining ingredients except flour and butter. Knead flour and butter together to make a roux. Add small portions of roux to sauce, whisking constantly until desired consistency is achieved.

Makes about 4 cups

THE OLD APPLE MILL RESTAURANT
3009 West Highway 76
Branson, MO 65616
(417) 334-6090
$–$$; □; C; (2)

47

Once upon a time, not so very long ago, a beautiful dark-eyed girl left her home in Greece and set off for Canada to attend law school. There she met and fell in love with a handsome Greek, who took her away from her dusty law books to live in his castle called New York City. So begins the story of Tom and Vasaliki (now called Bessy) Haldoupis.

Tom and Bessy had lived in New York for two years when a friend of Tom's convinced him to move to Springfield, Missouri. "I cried for two years after we moved here," says Bessy. "But you must realize that Springfield was not the city it is today. Such a little town it was, and after living in New York . . . ahhhh."

The pair opened a restaurant in Springfield called Cosmos, which soon became one of Springfield's most popular gathering places. Tom was the cook and Bessy ran the business. The menu featured recipes handed down from Bessy's mother, grandmother, and mother-in-law. Although the food was excellent, one of the main reasons people came to Cosmos was the warm welcome they received from Bessy. They may have entered as strangers, but they left as friends.

During this time, Tom remained enlisted with the merchant marines. When it looked like he might be called back to active duty, they sold Cosmos and prepared to move to Florida. Tom was released instead of re-called, so he and Bessy began looking for another restaurant location in the area. They found one thirty miles from Springfield in Reeds Spring, Missouri. "It was a little house with a bait shop attached," says Bessy. "We took out the bait shop and opened a ten-table deli. My son wanted to name it after his grandfather, so we called it Papouli's, meaning *grandfather* in Greek." Papouli's popularity soared, and within a year the deli grew into a full-fledged restaurant.

The menu still offers traditional family recipes with specialties like *mousaka*, a delicious blend of ground beef, eggplant, and potatoes topped with a creamy béchamel sauce. The *pastizio*, a hearty meat and macaroni pie encased in a light phyllo crust, is a visual and gastronomic master-piece. The roast leg of lamb presents a succulent delicacy flavored with Tom's secret spices. Two of the most popular desserts, Greek *baklava* (a scrumptious pastry full of nuts and calories) and *galactoboureko* (a deli-cious custard and phyllo dough concoction), may be difficult to pro-nounce but so easy to eat!

This tale's prince and princess are now living happily ever after in Reeds Spring. When you visit, you'll receive royal treatment.

Mousaka

2 pounds very lean ground beef
3/4 cup (1-1/2 sticks) butter
1/2 cup dry white wine
1/4 teaspoon oregano
1/4 teaspoon parsley leaves
Garlic powder to taste
Salt and pepper to taste
1 (28-ounce) can crushed tomatoes, drained
3 large potatoes
1/4 cup bread crumbs
2 medium eggplants

Preheat oven to 350 degrees. Brown ground beef in 4 tablespoons butter. Pour in wine, then add oregano, parsley leaves, garlic powder, salt, pepper, and drained tomatoes. Let simmer until all liquid is absorbed. Set aside.

Boil potatoes until half cooked. When cooled, peel, slice, and lightly brown potatoes in 4 tablespoons butter. Grease a 13-by-9-inch pan and cover with bread crumbs. Layer potatoes in bottom of pan. Drain excess fat off meat and spoon mixture over potatoes. Slice eggplant lengthwise and brown pieces in 4 tablespoons butter. Lay eggplant slices on top of meat. Pour *Béchamel Sauce* over casserole, covering entire top. Place on middle rack of oven and bake for 1 hour or until top turns golden brown.

Serves 8

Béchamel Sauce

1/2 cup (1 stick) butter
3 tablespoons flour
1 quart milk
3 eggs, beaten
1/2 cup grated Parmesan cheese
Pinch of nutmeg

On low heat, melt butter in a saucepan, then mix in flour, stirring constantly. Continue stirring while adding milk. Pour beaten eggs into mixture, then add Parmesan cheese and nutmeg, stirring well.

Makes about 4 cups

PAPOULI'S
Highway 248 and Reeds Springs Junction
Reeds Spring, MO 65737
(417) 272-8243
$–$$; □; C; (8)

"**P**raise the Lord and pass the ammunition," sang Spike Jones. But in this case, better substitute "biscuits," because the biscuits are one of the best reasons to visit this restaurant. Made from scratch, dripping with melted butter and sticky honey, if the biscuits don't get your adrenalin flowing, then the Big Band sound of Benny Goodman or Harry James playing nostalgically in the background will.

Decorated in a delightful 1940s motif, with black-and-white tiled floors and perky striped curtains, the memorabilia adorning the walls of Pass the Biscuits could rival a museum collection. The decor artfully combines Betty Grable–style shoes and Joan Crawford–type dresses with authentic newspapers proclaiming the end of World War II.

Even the menu resembles that of a 1940s diner, complete with an Uncle Milty's BLT on toast. For the diet-conscious starlet, the Greta Garbo features a grilled chicken breast with sliced tomatoes and cottage cheese. If your appetite is as big as Fibber McGee's closet, the grilled cheese and bacon sandwich with chips and creamy coleslaw should fill you up. Will Rogers never met a man he didn't like, and he would certainly be impressed with the hickory chicken and cheddar cheese sandwich named in his honor.

The concept was the brainchild of Terry Borden, a young man who spent his "rock and roll years" listening to Big Band music. Terry, whose background is marketing, married Lisa Gibbs, a third-generation restaurateur, and together they created this melodic blend of foods and moods. "The original idea for the biscuits," says Terry, "was to have our baker toss them to the customers. We found out the hard way that biscuits don't toss well. You may throw a biscuit, but you catch a handful of crumbs." The compromise was an open-air bakery where early risers can watch the biscuits and delicious assorted pastries being made.

In addition to '40s memorabilia, Pass the Biscuits displays a huge collection of autographed celebrity photos. They've even immortalized a window, broken and autographed by Howard Morris, who portrayed the rambunctious Ernest T. Bass on "The Andy Griffith Show."

Whether you drop in for a star-studded sandwich or partake of the tasty breakfast or dinner buffet, your sentimental journey to Pass the Biscuits is sure to be an enjoyable one. Clark Gable will be waiting for you, open face with tender roast beef, mashed potatoes, and gravy.

Chicken Potpie

4 cups cubed cooked chicken
1 (10-ounce) package frozen peas
   and carrots, cooked and drained
1/4 cup chopped onion
1/2 cup chopped fresh mushrooms
1/4 cup (1/2 stick) margarine
1/3 cup flour
1/2 teaspoon salt
1/4 teaspoon pepper
1 tablespoon instant chicken
   bouillon granules
2 cups water
3/4 cup milk
Enough biscuit dough for 6 large
   biscuits

Preheat oven to 450 degrees. Sauté onions and mushrooms in margarine until tender. Stir in flour, salt, and pepper. In a separate bowl, dissolve bouillon in water, then add along with milk to mushroom and onion mixture. Stirring occasionally, cook over medium heat until sauce starts to thicken, then simmer for 2 additional minutes. Add cooked vegetables and chicken and heat until bubbly. Pour into a 12-by-7-by-2-inch baking dish and top with biscuit dough. Bake for 10 to 12 minutes or until biscuits are lightly browned.

Serves 6–8

PASS THE BISCUITS
3524 Keeter Street
Branson, MO. 65616
(417) 335-8534
$; □; C; (3)

Peppercorns is undoubtedly one of the most attractive restaurants on "the strip." Fashioned after a Victorian country manor, its gabled roof, bay window, and wide veranda offer a most inviting site on a warm summer day.

Once inside, the French country decor surrounds guests in soothing shades of pink. The Gazebo room, open on three sides, along with the pitched ceiling gives the restaurant a light, airy feeling. Your sense of sight and smell are immediately stirred by appealing fresh pastries displayed near the front door. All in all, once you've entered Peppercorns you forget that one of the busiest highways in the United States lies just fifty yards away.

Peppercorns lays out a breakfast buffet that features homemade cinnamon rolls just like your favorite aunt used to make. For the lunch and dinner buffet, five featured entrees may include an out-of-this-world ham steak, barbecue ribs, or tasty charbroiled pork chops. There is always a fresh fruit and salad bar with hot homemade soup and tempting desserts.

The breakfast, lunch, and dinner menus present a variety of selections reasonably priced and attractively served. The dinner menu features a baked rainbow trout almondine, glazed with butter and served on a bed of rice. The specialty of the house is peppercorn chicken, dusted with fresh cracked peppercorns and sauteed with onions, bell peppers, and fresh mushrooms. The prime rib reigns as one of the best you'll find anywhere. One thing is certain: whether you try the buffet or order off the menu, you won't go away hungry!

Kevin Laughlin, president of the company and one of the youngest restaurant executives in the Branson area, is an expert at his craft. In the food service business for twelve years, he began as a line cook at McDonald's and now manages three Branson restaurants simultaneously. Kevin credits his grandmother, who was kitchen manager at Rock Lane Resort for twenty years, for teaching him everything he knows. "My grandmother set very high standards. She believed that the customer always came first, and that is a practice that I intend to continue. She also taught me that family is very important. My mom and dad, wife, and several aunts and uncles work for me as well."

Kevin is sought out numerous times each day by customers complimenting him on the restaurant's food and service. To each patron, Kevin turns his boyish smile and says, "Well, we want you to come back next time you visit Branson." They will!

Peppercorns' Shrimp Delight

16 jumbo shrimp, peeled and
    deveined
3 cloves garlic, peeled and split
1/4–1/2 cup light cooking oil
1 cup peeled and diced tomatoes
1/2 cup diced celery
1-1/2 cups ketchup
4 tablespoons sugar
2 teaspoons lemon juice
2 teaspoons sesame seeds
2 dashes of pepper
Yellow or white rice, cooked
    (4 servings)
Chopped green onions to garnish

Heat a wok or frying pan. Rub garlic on bottom and sides, then discard pieces. Pour in oil, heat, and sauté shrimp until tender. Add tomatoes and celery and cook for about 5 minutes. Stir in ketchup, sugar, lemon juice, pepper, and sesame seeds. When hot, pour over rice and garnish with chopped green onions.

Serves 4

PEPPERCORNS
2421 West Highway 76
Branson, MO 65616
(417) 335-6699
$–$$; □; C; (2)

53

Just outside the entrance to the Pier Restaurant, mounted in a gold-leaf frame, is a 1992 Five Star Diamond Award presented by the American Academy of Restaurant Sciences in their annual "Best of the Best" competition. Restaurants from all fifty states were judged on food quality, taste, service, and other criteria. When the votes were in, the Pier became one of only fifty to receive this coveted award in the Resort Restaurant category. Stepping inside the restaurant shows why.

In an atmosphere of muted blues, a tuxedoed maître d' escorts you to your table. Candlelight accentuates the exquisite view of Table Rock Lake and the surrounding Ozark Mountains. The menu tempts diners with a delightful assortment of entrees, including steaks, seafood, and poultry.

The steak au poivre is a tender Kansas City strip seared in olive oil with black peppercorns and served with a delicious Madeira sauce. Tournedos Oscar provides an enticing combination of beef medallions, crabmeat, and a rich béarnaise sauce. Shrimp milanaise weds garlic butter, espagnole sauce, and a creamy hollandaise. If you prefer something that you can pronounce, try the prime rib or cold water lobster. Both are superb! The red snapper, catfish, and salmon, all delivered fresh daily and prepared with a fine touch of seasonings, exquisitely satisfy a taste for fish.

Head chef and manager Bob Nicol has been practicing the art of fine dining for over twenty years. When Bob and his wife moved to the area in 1974, he saw a need for a high-quality restaurant and opened the first Wooden Nickel. After selling it and moving to Hot Springs, Arkansas, he next opened the popular South Shore restaurant. Nine years later, he decided to return to the Ozarks. Accompanied by his head chef from South Shore, Bob settled in and took over management of the Pier. Through the years Bob has employed and trained many of the chefs and restaurant managers in the area, which begins to explain such an abundance of good restaurants in and around Branson.

Although primarily known for its intimate fine dining, the Pier often hosts weddings receptions, anniversary parties, and other large functions. As a guest courtesy, the restaurant offers a boat dock and shuttle service if you choose to arrive by water.

The Pier proudly boasts, "The only thing we overlook is the lake," and true to its word, the food, service, and view are all exceptional. Make sure the Pier is one that you don't overlook.

Veal Normandy

4 (6-ounce) veal scallops (sliced
  from the leg)
1 cup flour, seasoned to taste with
  salt and pepper
1/2 cup (1 stick) butter
1/2 cup apple brandy
1 cup peeled and diced apple
1-1/2 cups heavy cream

Pound veal scallops with a mallet to
tenderize and lightly coat with seasoned flour. Melt butter in a sauté pan
and add veal and apple pieces. Sauté
until veal becomes browned on both
sides. Drain off butter, then add apple
brandy and cream to pan. Continue
cooking until sauce thickens. Serve
immediately.

Serves 4

PIER RESTAURANT
Kimberling Inn Resort and Conference Center
Highway 13, Kimberling City Shopping Center
Kimberling City, MO 65686
(417) 739-4311
Reservations recommended
$–$$$; □; C–D; (10)

55

THE PLANTATION

In 1983 two brothers, Leon and Don Kirkland, moved to Branson from Wichita, Kansas, and decided to open a restaurant. "Keep in mind," says Don, "the only thing we knew about a restaurant was how to read a menu. But we thought, if we run it like a business, surely it will succeed."

The pair hired a good kitchen and restaurant manager, but he soon got hit by Cupid's arrow and left the area. Don took over the kitchen and claims he had to learn quick because almost overnight, the restaurant had taken off. "When we opened the restaurant, we specialized in the 'all you can eat' plan," explains Don. "We had a sign that said, 'No one ever goes away hungry.' We still cater to that idea, and that's what keeps people coming back. We also serve good-quality home-style food."

Don and Leon obviously were doing something right, because for three years running The Plantation was voted the number one restaurant in Branson in a visitor's magazine poll, and it won each time on write-in votes. The establishment continually ranks in the top five in the Silver Dollar City public opinion survey.

Catering to public demand is what The Plantation does best. The breakfast/brunch buffet offers a great start to your day. Even late risers can get eggs, bacon, ham, and other delectable breakfast staples. The buffet serves up over forty items, including five meat choices like tender barbecue ribs in a zesty sauce or delicious smoked ham steaks. The selection always encompasses numerous vegetables and salads and a wide variety of fruits.

The dinner menu (if you don't opt for the buffet) offers seafood choices like juicy deep-fried scallops and shrimp. For fish lovers, the broiled fresh trout tastes like it just jumped out of Lake Taneycomo. The chicken cordon bleu is a succulent breast of chicken topped with Canadian bacon, Swiss cheese, and The Plantation's own luscious cheese sauce. Although Don claims they're not noted for their steaks, they certainly serve a lot, each one fork-cutting tender. The specialty is, of course, all-you-can-eat fried chicken and catfish, and the cooks stay busy keeping up with the demand.

Now that Leon has retired from the business, Don has gotten other family members involved. His wife, Noela, often greets the customers with her friendly smile and warm manner. Two nieces and a nephew work here as well. Even with all his family participating, Don still finds little leisure time. There are new additions to build and redecorating to do in the winter months when they're closed. "I've always wanted to winter in Hawaii," says Don, "just lay back and get lazy."

But as long as there's a tourist left in Branson, the beaches of Hawaii will have to get along without him.

56

Plantation Cornbread Dressing

2 small boxes cornbread mix
1 package hamburger buns
4 eggs, beaten
4 cups warm chicken broth
2 cups chopped celery
2 cups chopped onions
1 cup water
4–6 tablespoons sage, to taste
Salt and pepper to taste

Preheat oven to 350 degrees. Prepare cornbread as directed and let cool. Break cornbread and hamburger buns into small pieces in large bowl. In a saucepan, cook celery and onions in water until tender. Drain and add vegetables to bread mixture along with seasonings. Mix thoroughly and pour into 13-by-9-inch baking dish. Bake for 45 minutes and serve.

Serves 10–12

THE PLANTATION
3460 West Highway 76
Branson, MO 65616
(417) 334-7800
$–$$; □; C; (3)

It's a warm July evening in the Ozarks. You've been to four shows in one day, walked up and down the strip, and have shopped 'til you're ready to drop. You're tired and hungry and want something good to eat. Then put some "Pzazz" in your life!

Located in exclusive Pointe Royale, Pzazz offers one of the most extensive menus in the area. Twenty different sandwich options entice diners with items such as a delicious Philly Cheese, piled high with mounds of prime rib and mozzarella. Entree selections satisfy the heartiest appetites with a variety of poultry, beef, and seafood, such as baked or blackened orange roughy. For something different, explore the selections under "A Change of Pace." There's a delectable veal piccata cooked in white wine and lemon butter and tender "roll your own" chicken fajitas grilled with green peppers and red onions. Pzazz also serves breakfast anytime.

If you prefer variety, sample the luncheon or dinner buffet—it always includes a wonderful soup, fresh bread, and a large salad and dessert bar featuring homemade cobblers and ice cream. The lounge, open seven days a week, features live entertainment nightly at 8:30. For feet not worn out by shopping, there's even a dance floor perfect for doing the Texas Two-Step or the Branson Boogie.

Now, if on that same warm July evening you walk into Pzazz and are greeted with chorus of "Jingle Bells," don't be too surprised. Owner Jack Hamilton celebrates his Christmas Day birthday whenever the mood strikes him. He even leaves the Christmas decorations up and lit 365 days a year.

Jack is not only a local restaurateur of some renown, he's also one of the local celebrities. Known to his colleagues as "Hairbreath Harry," he spent sixteen years pitching for major league baseball teams like the Philadelphia Phillies, the Detroit Tigers, and the Chicago White Sox. A right-handed pitcher with a 95 m.p.h. fastball, he received his nickname because of the many close decisions on his pitches.

Jack moved to Branson in 1985 and opened up Jack's Club House, playing on his name. "I wanted to give people decent food at a decent price," he says. When the Pointe Royale location became available, Jack closed the Club House and opened Pzazz. "I've always like the name. It's short and simple and sticks with you."

Jack's a man of few words, but he'll always take the time to say "hi" and, if you'd like, spend some time talking about his illustrious baseball career. He may have concentrated on strikes when he was playing baseball, but he hit a home run when he opened Pzazz.

Jack's Cheesy Beefy Chowder

3 ounces sliced, smoked beef, cut
   into small chunks
1 stalk celery, finely chopped
1 medium onion, finely chopped
2 tablespoons butter or margarine
3 tablespoons flour
1/4 teaspoon salt
1/4 teaspoon dried basil
3 cups milk
3/4 cups shredded American
   cheese
1 tablespoon parsley flakes

In a medium saucepan, sauté celery and onion in butter until onion is tender. Blend in flour, salt, and basil, followed by pieces of beef. Add milk all at once. Simmer until mixture is thickened and bubbly, stirring frequently. Add cheese and stir until melted, then stir in parsley.

Serves 6–8

PZAZZ
Pointe Royale
#2 Highway 165
Branson, MO 65616
(417) 335-2798
$–$$; □; C; (4)

RIVERSIDE INN

Colored lights reflect off the Finley River as it slowly meanders past the Riverside Inn. A few guests are enjoying an after-dinner drink on the patio while piano music softly kisses the gentle night breeze. Slowly, almost as if unfolding in a mist, the pages of time turn back to the early '20s, when the Riverside Inn was built.

It was a time of sleek cars, flappers, and powdered knees. A time when the Charleston raged and so did Prohibition. A young art student, Howard Garrison, was entranced by the era and set out to become a part of it. He built a secluded little restaurant whose main attraction wasn't the delicious fried chicken, but a gambling and bootlegging operation he set up in the crowded little dining room.

Eventually these "illicit" pastimes came to the attention of a federal prosecutor, who promptly closed down the operation. But by then, the restaurant had earned a reputation for the best fried chicken around and soon reopened for legitimate business. As its popularity grew, so did the building itself. Other rooms were added until the restaurant became a maze of dining rooms, each more intriguing than the next.

Today Howard Garrison's influence is still apparent. His paintings hang throughout the establishment, and his murals have been left intact in the original dining area. Many of the original furnishings remain as well.

Present owner Eric Engle brought an air of refinement when he purchased the Riverside Inn. Although fried chicken remains the specialty, the chef prepares an excellent chateaubriand for two. The exquisite canard à l'orange presents a succulent half duck basted in honey and served with a delicious orange sauce. Other delicacies include a grilled lamb loin with tangy mint sauce, as well as frog legs battered and simmered in white wine, mushrooms, lemon, and butter. The extensive wine list complements every meal.

The Inn's desserts make you wish you had never heard the word "diet." Homemade vanilla ice cream arrives in a light pecan praline cup. The decadent chocolate mousse torte displays several different kinds of chocolate, topped with Kahlúa. The German chocolate cake and homemade raspberry ice cream offer exceptional temptations as well.

The Riverside Inn is located in Ozark, a little off the beaten path, but the exceptional food more than compensates for the drive. Besides, who knows where the magic of the evening may take you?

Lobster Thermidor

6 small lobster tails, cooked
3 cups half-and-half
4 egg yolks
1/2 cup sliced mushrooms
1-1/3 teaspoons salt
1/3 teaspoon nutmeg
3/4 teaspoon dry mustard
Dash of pepper
2 cups (4 sticks) butter, softened
1-1/3 cups flour
1/4 cup dry sherry
3 tablespoons lemon juice
1/4 cup grated Parmesan cheese,
   plus additional for topping
Paprika to garnish

Preheat oven to 350 degrees. In a large bowl, whip half-and-half, egg yolks, mushrooms, salt, nutmeg, dry mustard, and pepper. Pour into a double boiler and heat until hot. Knead softened butter and flour together to make a roux. Drop by spoonfuls into sauce mixture, whisking constantly. After sauce thickens, remove from heat and add sherry, lemon juice, and Parmesan cheese. Set aside.

Cut through tops of lobster tails lengthwise and remove all meat. Reserve shells. Cut meat into large chunks and add to sauce. Mix well and stuff mixture back into shells. Transfer shells to a baking dish, sprinkle with additional Parmesan cheese and paprika, and bake until golden brown, about 10 minutes.

Serves 6

RIVERSIDE INN
From Branson go north on Hwy. 65,
exit east on Business Rte. 14,
and follow signs to Finley River
Ozark, MO 65721
(417) 485-7566
Reservations recommended
$$–$$$; □; C–D; (13)

61

ROCK LANE RESORT

"This has got to be one of the best breakfasts that I've ever eaten," Jed Clampett (also known as Buddy Ebsen) was quoted as saying of the Rock Lane Resort restaurant. In fact, all of the "Beverly Hillbillies" cast stayed at the resort and were regulars at the restaurant while filming a portion of their 1966 season at Silver Dollar City.

Rock Lane originated back in the '50s as a privately owned weekend fishing getaway. In 1965 it opened to the public as a resort and until 1972 was the only one of its kind in the Branson area. Because of its uniqueness, Rock Lane became a popular retreat for numerous celebrities. Eddie Albert, Martin Milner, Bishop Bernard Law, and Dolly Parton, among others, all have been guests here.

Nestled on sixteen acres, the resort sits at the end of a peninsula on Indian Point with a quarter mile of shoreline. Sweet gums, oaks, and cedars dot the hill on which it stands, giving the place a secluded feeling while only a few minutes from Branson. Rock Lane also boasts the only full-service marina on Table Rock Lake.

The restaurant offers an almost unobstructed view of the beautiful lake below. Done in pink and teal, it's a lovely place to eat a leisurely meal and watch the colorful array of boats cruise by.

The chef and restaurant manager take a great deal of pride in the food as well as its presentation. They also stock the wine cellar with a wide variety, especially chosen to complement the menu. Dinner selections range from a delicious raspberry chicken sautéed in Grand Marnier to various succulent steaks, each cooked to perfection. One of the house specialties is medallions of beef sautéed in a rich brown sherry sauce with fresh garlic and mushrooms. The tenderloins are so tender, you can cut them with a fork.

At breakfast a huge, beautifully appointed buffet appears, laden with bacon, eggs, and a tempting assortment of fresh fruits. Menu choices include fluffy cheese omelets, a large portion of French toast sprinkled with powdered sugar, and fresh-ground Colombian coffee. The luncheon menu offers sandwiches for every appetite, each plate piled high with French fries.

When you eat at Rock Lane, you'll discover the secret of the Ozarks; beautiful vistas, delicious food, and wonderful places to visit.

Applebird Chicken

8 (6–8-ounce) boneless, skinless
chicken breasts
3 tablespoons butter oil
1 cup applejack brandy
2 apples cored and sliced into
1/4-inch wedges
16 slices Canadian bacon or ham
8 slices Swiss or Monterey Jack
cheese
Dill weed to garnish

Preheat oven to 450 degrees. Dredge in *Flour Seasoning* and set aside. Heat butter oil in sauté pan until hot. Sauté chicken until cooked on both sides, about 4 minutes. Add brandy (careful of flames) to chicken and simmer for 1 or 2 minutes, turning once. Sauce will thicken as it simmers. Remove chicken from pan and place on plates. Lay 2 pieces of Canadian bacon on top of each chicken breast and arrange apple slices on each side to form a "wing" effect. Place a slice of cheese on top of each and place in oven until melted. Sprinkle with dill weed and serve.

Serves 8

Flour Seasoning

3 cups flour
2 tablespoons salt
2 tablespoons course pepper
1 tablespoon garlic powder

Combine ingredients in a shallow bowl and set aside.

Makes about 3 cups

ROCK LANE RESORT
Indian Point Road
Branson, MO 65616
(417) 338-2211
$–$$; □; C; (6)

ROCKY'S ITALIAN RESTAURANT

If you walk into this restaurant and ask to speak to Rocky, manager and chef Duane Hertz will laugh and tell you, "Rocky isn't the owner's name—it's the state of his financial affairs." Yet from the line outside the front door you can tell that business is booming.

Located in downtown Branson, Rocky's is one of the busiest places in the area at lunch and dinner, and most of the customers are locals. More major "deals" have been executed in this pub than in all the Branson boardrooms put together. One of the reasons is the atmosphere that owner Chuck Barnes has created.

Rocky's consists of three rooms, but the bar is the place to dine if you want to get the Branson "feel." Reminiscent of an English pub, the room's wooden beams and exposed stone lend a cozy ambience. Dart boards hang on one wall, and mirrors and stained glass emblazoned with different brands of beer and liquor hang on the others.

The original building was erected sometime between 1900 and 1920; no one seems quite sure of the exact date. Another room was added on in the '30s, and the '40s saw the place converted into a feed mill and grocery store. Chuck bought the building in 1978 and turned it into a wholesale fishing tackle outlet. "It was sinful the amount of money I made . . . and tragic the amount I lost," he laughs. "A friend of mine and I had been talking about opening a restaurant, so one morning at 5:30 I got him out of bed, and two hours later we had a hole banged in the wall where I was going to put the counter. The name of my first place was Two Guys' Burgers and Fries . . . real original."

A couple of years later, Chuck decided he couldn't stand the heat in the kitchen (sometimes topping 126 degrees). Because he liked Italian food, he decided to open an Italian restaurant and thus evolved Rocky's. The bill of fare comes straight from Italy, with the exception of a Kansas City strip steak. The canneloni, bursting with meat and cheese, sets the mouth watering, as does the seafood fettuccine. Daily luncheon specials like lasagna and spaghetti marry a blend of cheeses and spices that is "magnifico." Every meal is served with a large salad and Italian bread.

"This restaurant consumes almost 24 hours of my day," says Chuck. "I work hard, but I've never had so much fun."

Veal Saltimbocca

2 (1-pound) whole veal tenderloins
1/2 cup flour
4 ounces prosciutto (Italian ham),
  julienned
8 ounces finely grated mozzarella
  cheese
Salt and pepper to taste
1/4 cup olive oil
1 cup dry white wine
1 clove garlic, minced
1 tablespoon chopped parsley
4 tablespoons butter

Preheat oven to 375 degrees. Remove sinew and fat from veal. Lay the loins lengthwise and slice into three equal strips. With grain facing up, pound medallions until nearly paper-thin. (Waxed paper placed over meat will prevent tearing during pounding.) After veal is flat, halve each piece for a total of 12 pieces. Dredge both sides in flour. Place veal on flat surface and sprinkle with ham and cheese. Roll each piece up jelly-roll style, secure with toothpicks, and sprinkle with salt and pepper.

Pour olive oil into a large skillet, just covering the bottom, and heat. Brown veal rolls on both sides and transfer to a baking dish. Bake for 10 minutes or until done.

Return skillet to medium-high heat and add wine to deglaze pan. Add garlic and parsley, and simmer for 1 minute. Add butter and turn off heat under pan. Work butter into wine mixture by shaking skillet from side to side. Remove toothpicks and pour sauce over veal rolls. Serve with pasta and red sauce or fettuccine Alfredo.

Serves 6

ROCKY'S ITALIAN RESTAURANT
118 North Sycamore
Branson, MO 65616
(417) 335-4765
$–$$; □; C; (1)

ROSE O'NEILL TEA ROOM

No trip to Branson would be complete without a visit to the College of the Ozarks, and no visit to the college would be complete without a stop at the Rose O'Neill Tea Room, especially for breakfast.

The staff here prepares fresh doughnuts, breads, and other pastries every morning. One of their giant cinnamon rolls and a cup of tea or coffee is almost a full meal. However, traditional breakfast eaters may want to try the "C of O" omelet or the hot pepper cheese omelet, both served with hashbrowns and toast or fluffy homemade biscuits.

Lunch and dinner are also a treat, especially when topped off with one of the delicious desserts. Selections include hot apple pie, lemon meringue pie (complete with sugar beads), or a dish of "Famous C of O Ice Cream" made fresh daily on the campus.

Skip Cobler, an alumnus of the college, manages the Rose O'Neill Tea Room. Like all College of the Ozarks students, he "paid" his tuition by working in one of the campus facilities. "My freshman year I worked in the laundry, and the only good thing I can say about the experience is that I met my wife there," he laughs.

Skip learned to cook by studying cookbooks and later trained with some of the country's top chefs. Today he teaches an average of ninety-two freshman each year who work in the tea room fifteen hours a week. "I get new faces each fall, and it seems that just when I have them trained as top-notch kitchen help or waitpersons, it's fall again and I have to start all over."

The tea room is located in The Friendship House just outside the college's main gate. In addition to the restaurant, the building houses a gift shop full of goodies that the students have made. Visitors can browse through a wide assortment of jellies, preserves, pottery, woven goods, and, at Christmas, a fruit cake so scrumptious that you'll eat it instead of using it for a door stop. Of course, there's a myriad of chubby Kewpie dolls for sale in honor of their creator, Rose O'Neill, a major benefactor to the school in the 1920s.

The Rose O'Neill Tea Room entertains its guests with Ozark-style home cooking at its best. Drop in and discover another one of the reasons so many people visit the area.

Friendship Doughnuts

6 cups lukewarm water
1-1/2 cups sugar
3 packages dry yeast
12 eggs, well beaten
1/4 cup light corn syrup
1-1/4 cups vegetable oil, plus
    additional for deep-frying
1 cup powdered milk
1 tablespoon salt
12 cups flour

In a large bowl, combine water, sugar, and yeast, and let stand for 1 minute. Add remaining ingredients, mixing in half the flour at a time. Knead into a soft dough, then cover and let rise until doubled (about 1 hour.) Punch dough down and roll out to 1/2-inch thickness. Cut out doughnuts and let double again. Deep-fry until golden brown, turning once. While doughnuts are hot, dip into **Glaze** and set on racks to cool.

Makes 18–20 large doughnuts

Glaze

1 (1-pound) box powdered sugar
1 cup hot coffee
1/2 tablespoon half-and-half

Pour powdered sugar into a bowl and slowly add liquids. (Note: The amount of hot coffee used will determine thickness of glaze.) Glaze should be thin enough to drizzle over doughnuts, but not watery.

Makes about 1-1/2 cups

ROSE O'NEILL TEA ROOM
The Friendship House
College of the Ozarks
Point Lookout, MO 65627
(417) 334-6411, Ext. 3341
$; □; C; (5)

SILVER DOLLAR CITY

Every highway leading to Branson is dotted with billboards extolling the wonders of Silver Dollar City. Some entice you with the myriad of music shows offered, and others assure you that from the minute you walk through the front gates, you'll enjoy a memorable experience that will last a lifetime. But the one sign sure to get your attention is that of a grandmotherly woman holding a gorgeous meringue pie, with the words "Come Hungry" emblazoned across the bottom.

Silver Dollar City is one of America's most popular theme parks and continually ranks in the top three for the quality of food it serves. Twenty-five restaurants and food venues appear throughout the park, each offering a "specialty of the house."

The Berries and Cream stand features fresh homemade ice cream topped with your choice of fresh strawberries or peaches. Flossie's Fried Fancies is the place to head for melt-in-your-mouth funnel cakes lavishly covered with one of four different toppings. Elmer's offers bratwurst, Polish sausage, or knockwurst topped with a generous portion of sauerkraut.

For a more leisurely meal, there are twelve dine-in restaurants from which to choose. Perhaps the most popular of these is the River Side Rib House, as celebrated for its open-air terraced dining area as it is for the marvelous barbecue. The delectable beef could make a Texan jealous. The half-slab of ribs and smoked chicken, slowly cooked in Silver Dollar City's own barbecue sauce, are what you'll be writing about on the postcards you send home.

Two restaurants not to miss, for the food as well as the historical significance, are Molly's Mill and Molly's Mine. Located on the site of an abandoned mine, these were established by Molly Brown herself in the late 1800s. Guests came not only for the delicious food, but to visit the unusual variety of dining rooms and the mine where the ghost of Molly's father purportedly roamed.

Today the restaurants still serve the same great home cooking that Molly did. Molly's Mill buffet offers genuine Ozark-style fried chicken and catfish and a savory turkey Creole. Diners also can choose from six different salads and a variety of fresh vegetables, breads, and desserts. Molly's Mine features a delicious ham and bean casserole, hearty beef stew, and corn spiced with red and green peppers.

Those with lighter appetites may seek out Mary's Pie and Sandwich Shop. The huge crab and tuna salad sandwiches, as well as the hot roast beef with mushrooms, are out of this world. However, be sure to leave room for dessert; the sight of the restaurant's scrumptious pies and cakes can make even a hard-core dieter fall off the wagon.

Terry Riddle, director of food and beverage services, supervises a staff of over 300, and each employee is dedicated to maintaining high quality standards. Silver Dollar City also boasts a graduate of the Culinary Institute of America as its executive chef.

Chef Doug "Moose" Zader came to Silver Dollar City from Denver in 1990. "I thought I'd add some culinary 'zip' to the food at Silver Dollar City," he laughs. "My first endeavor was to change the green beans offered in Molly's Mill. I prepared fresh green beans with onions and mushrooms and a splash of lemon. After adding them to the buffet, I was asked, 'Where are the *real* green beans?' I didn't realize that my fancy green beans were not only not appreciated, nobody liked them." Needless to say, the home-style green beans are back on the buffet.

Doug enjoyed a successful career as executive chef at the Stouffer's Hotel and Theater Cafe in Denver, but feels that he has finally found his niche at Silver Dollar City. "I like the attitude of the executives here," says Doug. "I have all sorts of credentials, but they didn't care how much I knew until they knew how much I cared. One of the first things I was told was 'If we're not proud of what we serve, we're not serving it.'"

One item that Doug successfully and proudly added to the menu was his buffalo chili. In 1991 he entered it in the Mickey Gilley Chili Cook-Off in Branson and won "Best New Chili Cooker." Buffalo chili tastes like beef chili, with less fat and a heartier consistency.

Silver Dollar City opened in 1960 as a diversion for visitors waiting to see Marvel Cave. Today it's undoubtedly the main attraction! With forty-six novelty shops, nine enchanting musical shows, fifteen exciting rides, over a hundred working craftspeople, and numerous excellent restaurants, it's no wonder Silver Dollar City is the number one tourist destination in the Midwest.

Hummingbird Cake

1 cup flour
1/4 teaspoon baking soda
1/2 cup sugar
1/4 teaspoon cinnamon
1 egg
1/4 cup vegetable oil
1/2 teaspoon vanilla extract
1/4 cup crushed pineapple,
    undrained
1/3 cup chopped pecans
1/2 cup mashed banana

Preheat oven to 350 degrees. Grease and flour three 9-inch cake pans. In a large bowl, combine flour, baking soda, sugar, and cinnamon. Add egg and oil, stirring until dry ingredients are moistened (don't beat). Stir in vanilla, pineapple, pecans, and banana. Pour batter into prepared pans and bake for 23 to 28 minutes, or until a toothpick inserted in the centers comes out clean. Cool cakes in pans for 10 minutes, then remove and let cool completely. Generously spread *Cream Cheese Frosting* on top of each, stack layers one on top of the other, and then finish with frosting on the sides.

Serves 10–12

Cream Cheese Frosting

2 cups powdered sugar
1-1/2 (8-ounce) packages cream
    cheese, softened
1/2 cup (1 stick) butter or
    margarine, softened
1 tablespoon lemon juice
1/4 cup chopped pecans

Sift powdered sugar into a bowl. Add cream cheese, butter, and lemon juice, and mix well. Stir in pecans and set aside until ready to use.

Makes about 4 cups

MARY'S PIE AND SANDWICH SHOP
Silver Dollar City
Branson, MO 65616
(417) 338-8100
$; no □; C; (6)

Turkey Creole

1-1/2 pounds cooked turkey
  breast, diced into 1/2-inch
  pieces
3 tablespoons margarine
2 cups diced onion
2 cups diced green bell peppers
1 clove garlic, minced
1/4 cup chopped parsley
1 tablespoon sugar
1 teaspoon salt
1 (2-1/2-pound) can crushed
  tomatoes, undrained
3/4 cup tomato juice
3/4 cup chicken broth
1 teaspoon basil
1 teaspoon pepper
1/2 teaspoon thyme
1 teaspoon Tabasco sauce, or to
  taste
White rice, cooked (6 servings)

In a large skillet, sauté onion, peppers, and garlic in margarine. Add remaining ingredients, except for turkey, and simmer for 1 hour, stirring occasionally. Add turkey and bring to a boil. Serve hot over rice.

Serves 6

MOLLY'S MILL RESTAURANT
Silver Dollar City
Branson, MO 65616
(417) 338-8100
$; □; C; (6)

71

Broccoli-Cauliflower Salad

1/2 pound fresh broccoli florets
1/2 pound fresh cauliflower florets
1/4 pound shredded cheddar
  cheese

Briefly blanch broccoli and cauliflower, then drain well. Add cheddar
cheese and toss well with *Peppercream
Dressing*. Serve chilled.

Serves 8

Peppercream Dressing

1/4 medium onion, finely diced
1 tablespoon minced garlic
1 tablespoon cracked pepper
1 teaspoon seasoned salt
1 tablespoon Tabasco sauce
1 tablespoon Worcestershire sauce
1 tablespoon red wine vinegar
1-1/2 tablespoons lemon juice
3 tablespoons grated Parmesan
  cheese
2-1/2 cups mayonnaise
1 tablespoon chopped chives
1/4 cup buttermilk
1/4 cup water

Combine ingredients and mix well.
Refrigerate until ready to use.

Makes about 4 cups

MOLLY'S MINE RESTAURANT
Silver Dollar City
Branson, MO 65616
(417) 338-8100
$; □; C; (6)

72

Joe's Baked Beans

1/4 pound cooked pork
1 pound navy beans, cooked
1-1/2 cups barbecue sauce
1/4 cup prepared mustard
1 cup molasses
1/2 cup brown sugar
1 small diced onion
1-1/4 tablespoons pepper

Preheat oven to 300 degrees. Combine all ingredients in a 3-quart baking dish and bake for 2 hours.

Serves 8–10

RIVER SIDE RIB HOUSE
Silver Dollar City
Branson, MO 65616
(417) 338-8100
$; no □; C; (6)

SUGAR HILL FARMS

While Sugar Hill Farms was being built, area residents would drive by and speculate about what the building would contain. It resembled an oversized doll village, trimmed with Victorian bric-a-brac and gingerbread. Even after the sign went up, speculation continued; just what was Sugar Hill Farms? To everyone's delight, the project turned out to be one of the most extraordinary restaurants in Branson.

The front dining room abounds with white wicker. The room is painted a cheery yellow and lilac, and three huge picture windows invite the sun in. The middle and back dining rooms are warm pink, with lots of homey knickknacks adorning the walls. Pink-clothed tables overlook an exquisite flower and herb garden.

If you ask to meet the owner, you'll know even before she introduces herself that she is the doll that belongs in this doll house. Joyce Sartin has bright blue eyes, a lilting voice, and an easy, appealing way about her. "I used to be known as the popcorn lady, and now I'm known as the pickle lady," she explains, referring to her past and present occupation. "I was the first to manufacture and market flavored popcorn. We had sixty different flavors."

After selling the company, Joyce and her husband Ron bought a farm in South Lead Hill, Arkansas. He set about planting hundreds of apple and peach trees, an assortment of other fruits, and a special variety of cucumbers, perfect for turning into pickles. While Ron farmed, Joyce began implementing a dream she had long harbored—that of opening her own restaurant.

The menu embraces recipes that Joyce has collected over the years, including her mother's pot roast and homemade bread. The luscious fruits and vegetables served are all grown on their farm. With such an abundance of produce, Joyce set up a canning operation in her specialty food shop at the north end of the building. The pastries in her pastry shop, just inside the front door, are all homemade and delicious, especially the tangy lemon-filled tarts and assorted cinnamon rolls drenched in sugary icing.

Sugar Hill Farms is a delightful place to spend a couple of hours. You can dine in the Garden Room, walk through the gardens, browse through the food shop, or sample the pastries. With the many additional plans Joyce has for Sugar Hill Farms, you can come back year after year and always find something new to try.

Beef Pot Roast

1 (3-pound) chuck, shoulder,
   brisket, round, or rump roast
1 teaspoon salt
1/2 teaspoon pepper
4 tablespoons flour
2 tablespoons shortening or
   vegetable oil
1 cup water

Preheat oven to 250 degrees. Wipe meat with a damp cloth. In a small bowl, combine salt, pepper, and flour. Rub onto entire surface of roast.

Melt shortening in a heavy skillet over high heat. Add meat and sear on all sides for 15 to 20 minutes. Remove meat from skillet and transfer to a roasting pan. Deglaze skillet with water, then pour mixture over roast. Cover and cook 1 hour and 45 minutes per pound, until meat is tender and well done. Serve with mashed potatoes and *Pot Roast Gravy*.

Serves 6

Pot Roast Gravy

3 medium onions, chopped fine
2 tablespoons butter
3 tablespoons cornstarch
1 teaspoon pepper
1 tablespoon chopped parsley
1 cup water
1 cube beef bouillon, crushed
Salt to taste

In a skillet or sauté pan, sauté onions in butter until transparent. Skim fat from roast broth and add to onions, followed by bouillon. Simmer for 30 minutes, then strain and return liquid to pan. Mix cornstarch, pepper, and parsley in water and pour into pan with seasoned liquid. Season with salt to taste, then allow to simmer for a few minutes until gravy thickens.

Makes about 1-1/2 cups

SUGAR HILL FARMS
Highway 165
Branson, MO 65616
(417) 335-3608
$-$$; □; C; (4)

TOM'S TOWN BAKERY

Traditions play an important role in the lives of the Ozark people. Trades and talents pass down from father to son, mother to daughter, generation after generation. George and Betty Roten passed on to their sons a talent for cooking, especially baking, and their younger son Tom has carried forth that tradition.

Tom begins his day as most townspeople are ending theirs. Working into the wee hours, he busily prepares dozens of tantalizing creations that will be consumed the next morning with steaming hot cups of coffee and glasses of frothy ice cold milk. For Tom, this schedule is more ritual than routine. "When I was a young boy, my dad would come into my bedroom at 3:30 in the morning and say, 'Get up Tom, it's time to go to work.' He and I would go down to his bakery, located in an old filling station across from the post office, and I'd help him make doughnuts."

Like his father before him, Tom makes his baked goods from scratch. In an area where supermarket bakeries seem to lead the competition, Tom has carved out his own niche. "I use more butter than shortening and real vanilla instead of imitation. I believe that if you're going to call something by a particular name, you shouldn't leave any doubt in the customer's mind what it is." As you look over the exquisite assortment in his display cases, there could be no doubt.

Tom's sticky buns reward those that bite into them with a wonderful yeast taste. They're oozing with a delicious cinnamon filling and piled high with tender fresh pecans. The layers of paper-thin dough in his crispy cinnamon swirls melt in your mouth. The cream cheese muffins, one of Tom's specialties, will make you swear there's a package of cream cheese in every one. Other favorites are the chocolate éclairs and cream puffs, each filled with a delightfully rich vanilla cream.

Not limited to pastries, Tom turns out a delicious assortment of fresh baked cookies—English toffee, chocolate chocolate chip, and chocolate chip pecan. His $15,000.00 Oatmeal Cookies took their name from a recipe that supposedly sold for $15,000.00 but which a fellow baker gave to Tom.

Small bakeries are going the way of the dinosaur, according to Tom. These days very few specialty shops do even 90 percent of their baking from scratch. Tom, though, is doing his part to ensure that the family tradition carries on. Among his six children, his eleven-year-old daughter has shown interest in becoming a third-generation baker.

Tom's Town Bakery, located downtown on Main Street, has been baking memories since 1983. Stop in and take a dozen home with you.

Tom's English Toffee Cookies

2-1/2 cups sugar
2 cups macaroon coconut (or
  process flaked coconut in a
  food processor until fine)
1/2 cup powdered milk
1 teaspoon baking soda
1 teaspoon salt
1/2 cup (1 stick) butter, softened
1-1/4 cups vegetable shortening
3 eggs
3-1/2 cups flour
3/4 cup English toffee pieces

Preheat oven to 375 degrees. In a
large bowl, combine sugar, coconut,
powdered milk, baking soda, salt, butter, and shortening. Cream until light.
Add eggs and mix until smooth. Add
flour, 1 cup at a time, and mix until
smooth. Add toffee pieces and mix
well. Dough should be fluffy and work
easily into 1-inch balls. Place balls on
cookie sheets and flatten tops slightly.
Bake for 8 to 9 minutes, then cool on
racks before serving.

Makes about 60 cookies

TOM'S TOWN BAKERY
111 West Main Street
Branson, MO 65616
(417) 334-2240
$; no □; C; (1)

77

TOMMY'S RESTAURANT AND LOUNGE

At the top of a sharp rise in the land where Highways 65 and 165 intersect sits a large, sprawling, two-storied building that offers a wonderful northwestern view of the famed "Branson Strip." On any given day, at most any given time, the parking lot teems with cars and tour buses. But the crowds are all part of the fun at Tommy's.

Like several others, this restaurant lays claim to the best buffet in Branson. It's undoubtedly right up there, with offerings like slow-cooked barbecued beef brisket, tangy sweet-and-sour chicken or shrimp, and a scrumptious cashew chicken. Hungry guests can top off the entrees with a trip to the dessert bar, which often features a special French apple cruet or homemade fruity cobblers. "Our buffet draws about 90 percent of our business," says Mike Morrissey, head chef and the owner's son. "A lot of the locals eat here every day because they know that there will be different offerings daily."

Mike, a self-taught cook, is an experimenter from way back, and the menu reflects his diversified tastes. He developed a blackened chicken with a creamy fettuccine and promises that "if you like Cajun food, you'll love this one." He sautés his walleye fillet in white wine and serves it with a sensational walnut butter. The baked onion soup au gratin contains so much cheese you might want to ask for your soup on the side. The best topper for one of Mike's meals is his extraordinary triple-chocolate cheesecake, so be sure to save room!

Besides the delicious food you'll also find some of the best new talent performing on stage here. Having long been known for the Monday night talent shows running from November to April, Tommy's can take credit for giving a leg up to many members of Branson's now-professional talent. Many well-known celebrities often show up at this Monday night rite to scout out new talent for their theaters.

Just inside the restaurant entrance is a "Walk of Fame" that displays numerous autographed photos, and some candid shots, of celebrities who have eaten at Tommy's. In addition, a large U.S. map on the wall invites visitors to mark their hometown with the pushpins provided. "We get so many visitors during the summer months that there are times my dad has to clear the map off daily," say Mike.

It was Mike's mother Marilyn who encouraged her husband, Tommy, to buy the restaurant. It was also her idea to keep the fifteen-foot Christmas tree up year-round and decorate it for each holiday. "Actually, she didn't have a place to store it," laughs Mike. "But the customers love seeing the tree decorated for the different holidays."

Tommy's Restaurant and Lounge is a delight anytime you get a chance to visit.

French Apple Cruet

4 medium Golden Delicious apples
1/2 cup (1 stick) butter
1/4 cup sugar, plus additional to
  garnish
8 egg roll wrappers or prepared
  crêpes
1 egg, beaten
Vegetable oil for deep-frying
Cinnamon to garnish

Peel, core, and slice apples into 1/4-inch pieces. In a small skillet, brown apples in butter and sugar for 5 minutes over medium-low heat. Set aside to cool.

Lay out wrappers or crêpes and spoon 2 tablespoons of cooked apples into the center of each. Spoon 2 tablespoons of *Cream Cheese Filling* next to apples. Turn bottom corner of wrapper up to cover filling. Fold in sides and finish rolling egg-roll fashion. Brush edges with beaten egg to seal. Deep-fry at 350 degrees for 2 minutes. Sprinkle with sugar and cinnamon and serve warm.

Serves 8

Cream Cheese Filling

1/2 (8-ounce) package cream
  cheese, softened
1 egg
1/2 cup sugar

Combine all ingredients and beat until smooth. Set aside until ready to use.

Makes about 1 cup

TOMMY'S RESTAURANT AND LOUNGE
Highway 65 and 165
Hollister, MO 65672
(417) 334-4995
$–$$$; □; C; (5)

UNCLE JOE'S BAR-B-Q

The secret of Uncle Joe's barbecue is almost an Ozark legend, which is kind of strange since the story began in Tennessee. Supposedly a man named Roy got a taste for some good barbecue while touring around that state. Following directions, he soon found himself on a dirt road somewhere out in the sticks. Finally, he came to a decrepit old building with the name "Uncle Joe's" hand-painted on the roof. Under normal circumstances, Roy probably would have hot-footed it out of there, but seeing that there were so many cars around the place, he stopped in and indeed found the best barbecue that he had ever tasted.

It was 1956 before Roy got around to opening his own place, but in those days barbecue wasn't as popular in Branson as it would become. So Roy succumbed to customer demand and turned the business into a front for selling "white lightning" imported all the way from Arkansas.

Over the years Roy's restaurant and Uncle Joe's sauce recipe changed hands quite a few times, but in 1971 Dick Biedenstein stepped in. He bought an old restaurant scheduled for razing and rebuilt it where Uncle Joe's stands today. Later he and his partner Maria Wilson constructed from scratch each table, chair, and booth in the cozy main dining room. "I know every piece of furniture intimately," laughs Maria. "I sanded and varnished each one. When the first table got a scratch on it, I thought I would die."

In 1990 Dick sold his half of the business to Maria in order to pursue another venture. Continuing their established reputation for quality, Maria selects the finest cuts of beef and pork to smoke slowly in a hickory-wood smoker. A beef brisket takes about twelve hours to cook to perfection; ribs take about six. The chicken is heat-cooked over the same hickory wood, producing some of the tastiest you'll ever find. One of the best items on the menu is the beef, pork, ham, and ribs combination, enough for Goliath but so delicious you'll eat every bite. Of course, Maria serves up all this mouth-watering meat with Uncle Joe's secret sauce on the side.

No barbecue would be complete without the beans and potato salad, and here you'll feast on some of the tastiest. The beans cook in a thick rich sauce, and huge chunks of smoked meat fill every spoonful. A tempting salad bar also features homemade soup—try the yummy cheddar vegetable or cream of potato.

Although originating in Tennessee, the Ozarks have adopted Uncle Joe's recipe as their own. And whoever Uncle Joe was, he sure made a powerful good barbecue.

80

Potato Salad

6 medium white potatoes, peeled,
  cooked, and diced
3 hard-boiled eggs, chopped
1 cup chopped onion
1-1/2 cups bottled Parmesan
  peppercorn salad dressing
1 teaspoon apple cider vinegar
1/4 cup prepared yellow mustard

In a large bowl, combine potatoes, eggs, and onions. Thoroughly combine remaining ingredients and stir into potato mixture. Chill for 2 hours and serve.

Serves 6–8

UNCLE JOE'S BAR-B-Q
2807 West Highway 76
Branson, MO 65616
(417) 334-4548
$–$$; □; C; (2)

In 1967, as Wayne Hargis was making deliveries in his Colonial Bread truck, he spotted a "for sale" sign on a restaurant at the intersection of Highways 165 and 76. He bought the restaurant and then went home to tell his wife. Fortunately for him, she was ready for a break from the ice cream stand she owned, where she hand-dipped twelve to fifteen gallons a day.

The new acquisition boasted forty seats (half were at the counter) and a drive-up window. The kitchen consisted of a four-foot grill, a broaster, and one deep-fryer, ready to turn out hamburgers made with 100 percent fresh ground beef and broasted chicken never before offered in Branson.

Within in a few years Wayne's Restaurant had become one of the area's most popular dining establishments. Meeting local demand meant moving, and so they relocated to their present spot on West Highway 76. The new place lacked the drive-up window but had a seating capacity of 120. Though the menu changed a little, the burgers and chicken remained the house specialties.

About this time young Kevin Hargis was introduced to the business. "I started busing tables when I was five," he recalls. "Eventually, they put me in the kitchen. I even remember Dad's excitement when he replaced his old grill with a new six-foot one. At one time or another, I think everyone who lived in Branson came in to eat, and my dad knew every one of them. In 1975 he became quite ill, and while he was in the hospital the restaurant burned down. The people of Branson were wonderful in their response. They set up donation funds all over town. A local lumber company donated the lumber and the plumbing was contributed as well. But I guess the biggest thing that was given was everyone's time. People came from all over offering their labor, and within a month the restaurant was rebuilt."

Today Kevin continues the traditions set by his father. A graduate of the Baltimore International Culinary Arts Institute, he still offers hamburgers and broasted chicken but has expanded the menu somewhat. You won't see a cordon bleu, but you will find some world-class chili and hearty beef stew. The deep-fried and secretly seasoned chicken livers and gizzards rival any Southern fried chicken recipe. In addition, Kevin has added homemade desserts like his creamy peanut butter pie and a wonderful raisin pecan pie.

Each year Kevin makes gallons of beef stew and chili and gives it to the Branson Fire Department for its annual fund-raiser. "In this small way, I'm trying to repay the people of Branson for what they did for my family so many years ago."

Vegetable Soup

10 cups beef stock or broth
4 celery stalks, diced
1 large onion, diced
1/2 small head of cabbage, diced
3 bay leaves
1/4 cup dried parsley
1 teaspoon coarse pepper
2 teaspoons garlic powder
1/2 tablespoon salt
1 (12-ounce) bag frozen mixed
  vegetables
1 (16-ounce) bag large-cut frozen
  vegetables
1 (16-ounce) can peeled tomatoes,
  chopped
1 (11-1/2-ounce) can V-8 or
  tomato juice

Pour 5 cups beef stock into a large pan or stock pot. Add fresh vegetables and seasonings. Simmer for 15 minutes or until vegetables are tender. Add frozen vegetables, tomatoes, juice, and remaining beef stock. Simmer for at least 15 minutes or until ready to serve.

Serves 8–10

WAYNE'S RESTAURANT
1915 West Highway 76
Branson, MO 65616
(417) 334-5482
$; no □; C; (2)

Down the road about a mile west of Silver Dollar City sits a rustic wooden building bearing the name "Wooden Nickel." You'll often see two or three tour buses parked out front and as many as thirty or forty cars, but don't let that deter you from going in. The wait's usually no more than five to seven minutes and well worth it.

The Wooden Nickel's fifty-odd menu items include a scrumptious prime rib, coated in a special seasoning and slow-cooked to perfection. The barbecue ribs are melt-in-your-mouth delicious and plentiful enough for one ravenous appetite or two just at the starving stage. The steaks are tender, juicy, and cooked exactly the way you like them.

If your taste runs to something lighter, the seafood selection is a fish lover's dream. Scallops arrive in a tangy lemon butter sauce, and the crab legs are big enough to make you wonder at the size of the original owner.

Owners Andy Bray and Ed Wall have constructed a visually intriguing restaurant, part of which is an old farmhouse original to the property. The most unusual feature of the establishment is the "salad tree bar"—a salad bar literally built around a 150-year-old living tree. "About a century and a half ago," explains Andy, "the farmer who built this farmhouse went outside his front door and planted himself this tree. Now most everyone thought that he planted it for shade, but I figure he knew that 150 years later this tree would be the perfect place for a salad bar."

Andy and Ed have a partnership that balances each other. Ed likes working with computers and measuring profit margins. Andy likes the one-on-one contact, and if you can ever get him to sit still long enough, he'll regale you with stories that will have you laughing 'til you cry.

Andy wanted to be a singer all his life, but he says that's not what brought him to Branson. ("I'm as tone deaf as a mud fence.") He insists that he invented lip-syncing, because to join a choir when he was younger he had to promise only to move his mouth while the rest of the choir sang. When asked what *really* brought him to Branson, Andy'll look you right in the eye and say "Greed."

Whatever it is that brings *you* to Branson, be sure to put Andy and the Wooden Nickel down as a "must visit."

Wooden Nickel Stuffed Mushrooms

30 large mushrooms, washed and stems removed

1/4 cup (1/2 stick) margarine, melted

1 (8-ounce) package cream cheese, softened

6 ounces crabmeat

1 tablespoon minced onions

8 drops Tabasco sauce

1 teaspoon salt

1 teaspoon white pepper

1 tablespoon Worcestershire sauce

Wild or yellow rice, cooked (6 servings)

Preheat oven to 350 degrees. Brush mushroom caps with melted margarine and place on a cookie sheet.

In a small bowl, combine remaining ingredients except rice and mix well. Divide and roll mixture into 30 balls and set aside.

Bake mushroom caps for 15 minutes or until done. Remove from oven and place 1 ball of cheese mixture into each cap. Return to oven for 10 to 15 minutes, or microwave on high for 1 minute. Serve warm on a bed rice.

Serves 6

WOODEN NICKEL
West Highway 76
Branson West, MO 65737
(417) 338-2737
$-$$$; □; C; (7)

RESTAURANT LOCATOR

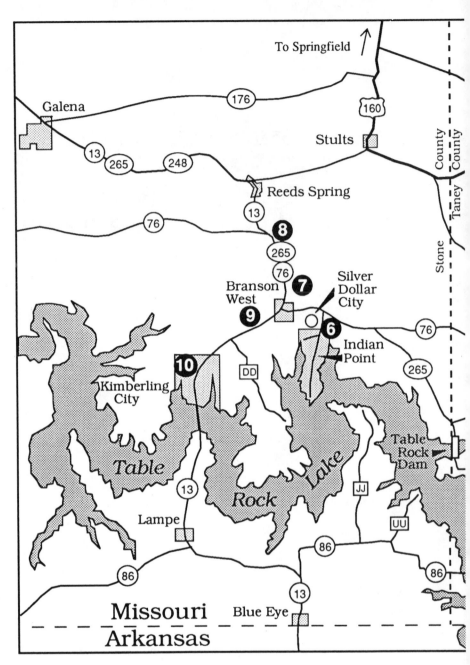

KEY
1 = Downtown, Highway 248, East Highway 76
2 = West Highway 76 to Highway 165/Gretna Road
3 = West Highway 76 past Highway 165
4 = Highway 165
5 = Point Lookout, Highway 165 and 65

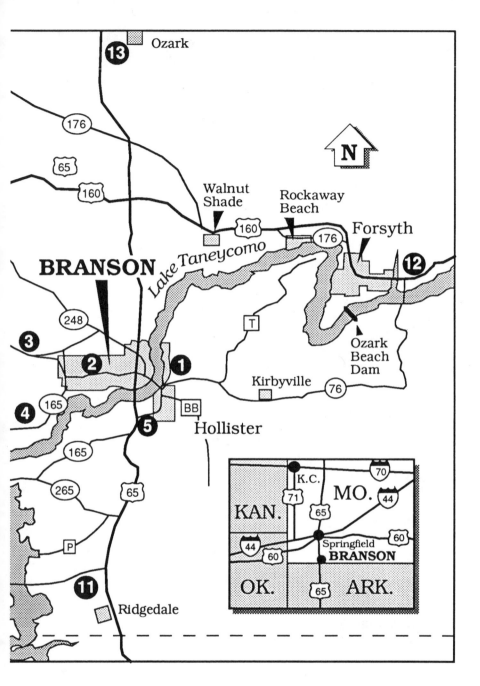

6 = Indian Point Road
7 = Branson West
8 = Reeds Spring
9 = Highway 13 and Stone Ridge
10 = Kimberling City

11 = Highway 86
12 = Forsyth
13 = Ozark

89

AREA RESTAURANT LOCATIONS

AREA 1 (Downtown, Highway 248, East Highway 76)
Branson Cafe
The Candlestick Inn
Dimitri's
Mel's Restaurant
Rocky's Italian Restaurant
Tom's Town Bakery

AREA 2 (West Highway 76 to Highway 165/Gretna Road)
Bob Evans General Store
Cakes and Creams Dessert House
Confetti's Restaurant
Donovan's Hillbilly Inn Restaurant
Duck Cafe
Garcia's Restaurant
The Old Apple Mill Restaurant
Peppercorns
Uncle Joe's Bar-B-Q
Wayne's Restaurant

AREA 3 (West Highway 76 past Highway 165)
Aunt Mollie's Cupboard
Pass the Biscuits
The Plantation

AREA 4 (Highway 165)
Buck Trent Breakfast Theater
Fall Creek Steak House
Pzazz
Sugar Hill Farms

AREA 5 (Point Lookout, Highway 165 and 65)
Rose O'Neill Tea Room
Tommy's Restaurant and Lounge

AREA 6 (Indian Point Road)
Mary's Pie and Sandwich Shop (Silver Dollar City)
Molly's Mill Restaurant (Silver Dollar City)
Molly's Mine Restaurant (Silver Dollar City)
River Side Rib House (Silver Dollar City)
Rock Lane Resort

AREA 7 (Branson West)
    The Brass Rail
    Wooden Nickel

AREA 8 (Reeds Spring)
    The Hungry Hunter
    Papouli's

AREA 9 (Highway 13 and Stone Ridge)
    Big Jim's Steak House
    Brier Patch Village
    Mary Jane's

AREA 10 (Kimberling City)
    Ahoys
    Pier Restaurant

AREA 11 (Highway 86)
    Chef Richard's Long Creek Cafe
    Devil's Pool Restaurant

AREA 12 (Forsyth)
    B & G Books & More

AREA 13 (Ozark)
    Riverside Inn

RESTAURANT INDEX

RECIPE INDEX

The **bold** asterisk (*) preceding a recipe title indicates a "recipe within a recipe"; that is, one that appears within the preparation instructions for a primary recipe but which, in some cases, could stand alone or be served with another favorite dish.

Mousaka, 49
*Béchamel Sauce, 49
Mt. Branson Rocky Road Cake, 23
*Rocky Road Frosting, 23
Peppercorns' Shrimp Delight, 53
Plantation Cornbread Dressing, 57
Potato Salad, 81
Pumpkin Cheesecake, 21
Seafood Mornay, 47
*Mornay Sauce, 47
Shepherd's Pie, 5
Sour Cream Raisin Pie, 41
Sticky Buns, 17
*Dough Coating, 17
*Goo, 17
Strawberry Soup, 43
Stuffed Ozark Catfish, 29
Tom's English Toffee Cookies, 77
Turkey Creole, 71
Veal Normandy, 55
Veal Saltimbocca, 65
Vegetable Soup, 83
Wooden Nickel Stuffed Mushrooms, 85

Susan St. Marie-Martin has worn many hats in her lifetime. As a country music entertainer, she had several chart records to her credit. Deciding that the "other side of the camera" was more to her liking, she went on to write and produce documentaries, training films, television commercials, children's television programming, and jingles.

A marketing, travel, and public relations professional, Susan now resides in Branson with her husband and two children.

ORDER FORM

ORDER DIRECT—CALL (800) 877-3119 OR FAX (816) 531-6113

Please rush the following book(s) to me:

_____ copy(s) **BRANSON COOKIN' COUNTRY** for $9.95 plus $2 shipping

_____ copy(s) **DAY TRIPS FROM SAN ANTONIO AND AUSTIN** for $8.95 plus $2 shipping

_____ copy(s) **DAY TRIPS FROM KANSAS CITY** for $8.95 plus $2 shipping

_____ copy(s) **KANSAS CITY GUIDE** for $7.95 plus $2 shipping

_____ copy(s) **KANSAS CITY CUISINE** for $12.95 plus $2 shipping

_____ copy(s) **MEMPHIS CUISINE** for $12.95 plus $2 shipping

_____ copy(s) **NASHVILLE CUISINE** for $12.95 plus $2 shipping

_____ copy(s) **SAN DIEGO CUISINE** for $12.95 plus $2 shipping

_____ copy(s) **DALLAS CUISINE** for $12.95 plus $2 shipping

METHOD OF PAYMENT

_____ Enclosed is my check for $_____ (payable to TWO LANE PRESS, Inc.)

_____ Please charge to my credit card: _____VISA _____ MasterCard

Acct. # _____

Signature _____

SHIP TO: _____   GIFT/SHIP TO: _____

_____   _____

_____   _____

_____   _____

_____   _____

_____   FROM: _____

MAIL COMPLETED ORDER FORM TO:

Two Lane Press, Inc. • 4245 Walnut Street • Kansas City, MO 64111